PHEASANT FOR AMATEURS:

A PRACTICAL HANDBOOK ON THE
BREEDING, REARING, AND GENERAL MANAGEMENT
OF AVIARY PHEASANTS.

BY

GEORGE HORNE.

ILLUSTRATED.

LONDON:
L. UPCOTT GILL, 170, STRAND, W.C.

PREFACE.

OF all the birds inhabiting these Islands, there is probably no bird that causes its owners the amount of care, trouble, and anxiety that the Common Pheasant does, no other bird affording the same amount of sport, and, I may add, causing so much poaching and misery. These remarks apply principally to our old variety; but during recent times, intercourse with other countries, and rapid means of transit, have enabled us to add to this one solitary variety numerous of the gorgeous pheasants of other climes, for the most part even far handsomer than our bird, and with constitutions hardy enough to stand our severest winters.

For many years I have been a most enthusiastic admirer of all pheasants, each year breeding several varieties, frequently in considerable number, and always on the look-out for any fresh introductions. I have corresponded with many others on the subject, collecting all the information possible, and have bought, sold, and exchanged, so as always to keep my stock at the very highest pitch of perfection; and the result of these experiences I now submit in the following pages, which I have endeavoured to render as explicit as possible.

I have never been a game-preserver in the common acceptation of the word; but if I were, the height of my ambition would be to see a score or two of those truly majestic birds, Reeves' (an adult male is fully 6ft. long), feeding from the home coverts towards my windows; he is an ornament to any grounds, and as easy to rear as a chicken.

GEORGE HORNE.

HEREFORD.

CONTENTS.

CHAP.		PAGE
I.—INTRODUCTION	. . . .	1
II.—AVIARIES AND COOPS	. . . . .	4
III.—BREEDING	. . . .	16
IV.—REARING	. . . .	28
V.—THE GOLD PHEASANT	. . . . .	34
VI.—THE SILVER PHEASANT	. . . .	37
VII.—THE LADY AMHERST PHEASANT	. . .	39
VIII.—THE SWINHOE PHEASANT	. . . .	42
IX.—THE SŒMMERRING PHEASANT	. . .	44
X.—THE REEVES' PHEASANT	. . . .	46
XI.—THE SIAMESE FIREBACK PHEASANT	. .	50
XII.—THE ELLIOT PHEASANT	. . . .	52
XIII.—THE VERSICOLOR, OR JAPANESE PHEASANT	.	54
XIV.—THE PEACOCK PHEASANT	. . . .	57
XV.—THE IMPEYAN PHEASANT	. . . .	59
XVI.—THE COMMON PHEASANT	. . . .	61
XVII.—THE CHINESE PHEASANT	. . . .	71
XVIII.—CROSSES, AND IMPORTING SPECIMENS	. .	74
XIX.—DISEASES, &c.	. . . . . .	77
XX.—CATCHING BIRDS, PACKING, &c.	. . .	82
XXI.—A WALK ROUND MY AVIARIES	. . .	84

Aviary Pheasants.

CHAPTER I.

INTRODUCTION.

Adaptability of Pheasants for Breeding and Rearing in Towns—The Best Varieties—Gold Pheasants: Beauty of; Keeping in the Open—No great Expense needed—Plan of Work.

PROBABLY there is no greater attraction in the grounds of a country house than a good collection of foreign pheasants; but it is not everyone who has a country house, and one of the chief merits of these birds is that, although they add greatly to the beauties of our gardens, still they may be kept by town residents, and even in the very limited space of most suburban houses some of our most beautiful varieties may be bred and reared. Take, for instance, the Gold and the Lady Amherst, two of the best. A small, lean-to shed, with a little inclosure—the whole, not more, say, than 6ft. by 12ft.—is ample for a pair.

As regards Gold, those persons who do not wish to breed them can always have a lovely pen of birds at a very moderate cost, by buying young cocks and letting them come to full plumage in their own aviaries. By so doing, they will have birds challenging the admiration of all. I generally have twenty, sometimes twenty-five, adult cocks in one aviary, and they are a glorious sight, with their almost ceaseless motions, as they dance round each other, first displaying their tippet or collar on one side and then on the other. These birds I keep in an open aviary—in fact, it is one of my large portable ones; it is placed in the carriage drive, exposed to every weather, and in a very cold situation, the ground being on the banks of the Wye, and facing hills which, from October, 1885, for nine months, were, I believe, not one week without snow. The birds roost in the open, and I am frequently amused by being asked "how I take them in of a night," &c. People seem to think that, because they are Chinese birds, they must be natives of a hot climate, and unable to bear cold, forgetting that there is plenty of cold as well as heat in China. I think that, bringing up birds as I do, and not coddling them, I get the "survival of the fittest;" in other words, my stock is strong and robust. As a matter of fact, I seldom lose a bird except from accident.

Much may be done with very small means. It was

upwards of twenty years ago when I first commenced breeding Gold pheasants; my space was very limited, but I contrived to rear a great many birds, and to prove the fallacy of what was then believed, viz., that birds of a year old would not breed. After a time, I purchased a pair of Lady Amhersts, giving £16 for them. I believe I was one of the earliest to breed these elegant birds, and for some years I was most successful. Next I went in for Reeves', Versicolors, Swinhoes, Firebacks, Impeyans, Peacocks, and lastly for our most recent importation, and the rarest and the handsomest of all, the Elliot.

In the following chapters I propose to give, as explicitly as possible, the plan I adopt for rearing and keeping the several varieties. The best forms of aviaries, setting-boxes, coops, runs or inclosures, the general management, &c., will be fully treated. After that, I intend to describe the most popular varieties, and to indicate any special treatment they require.

I take it for granted that few persons would think of commencing pheasant-breeding later than June. I do not say a pair of Gold pheasants, for example, obtained as late as that, would not breed, but the chances are greatly against their doing so. It is recommended to obtain the birds early in the spring, and not to defer it till the season is far advanced, for the birds then never settle down so well.

CHAPTER II.

AVIARIES AND COOPS.

Permanent Aviaries: Soil on which to Erect; Shape and Dimensions; Drainage; Plants for; Perches; Cleaning; Water—Hardiness of Pheasants—Portable Aviaries: Dimensions; Cost—Portable Aviaries for Young Birds — Coops: Advantages of Bottom Boards in; Changing Soiled Boards.

PERMANENT AVIARIES.

THERE is no doubt that the best soil for permanent aviaries is a dry gravel, and about the worst a stiff clay. Much will depend on the purse and taste of the fancier, and the situation available. There is no better form of aviary than that of an ordinary shed, with span roof (see Fig. 1); it can be made as ornamental as you please. Make the back 6ft. high, the front the same, 12ft. back to front, and 12ft. wide; this is a good size for such birds as are usually kept in aviaries. Put a span roof over this, sloping to back and front; board the back and the top half of the front, and put netting over the rest, so that only one quarter of the roof is open, and that the lower front portion; felt the whole of the

Fig. 1.—Permanent Span-roof Aviary.

boarding, and well tar. I have left it to choice whether the aviary have a brick back—say a garden wall—or be weather-boarded. If you can put both back and front on brick footing, all the better. It is desirable that there should be a drain in front—merely a dug-out pit, with brick sides and grating; no rats can then work up the drain, and the water will soak away. If you have a high back wall, the roof may slope from back to front. On the front footing put light upright quarterings, 2ft. 8in. apart, centre to centre; the wall plate rests on them. Wire with 2ft. 6in. netting, 1in. mesh. If the netting is run lengthways, the rafters may be wider apart. The doors should each be about 2ft. wide. Board the front at bottom with two 11in. boards, and fill above them with netting; this prevents cats and dogs being seen. The wire partitions between the aviaries may be of larger mesh, but should be boarded about 2ft. high at bottom, to prevent the cocks fighting.

Plant shrubs and creepers in front, to break the wind. For the interior, dig out all the soil for 6in., and fill in with concrete; above this place rough gravel, with fine sand on top. By this means you never have tainted ground. All impurities get washed out into the drain, if that is properly laid. Occasionally, remove all the gravel, &c., and replace it with clean. This, bear in mind, is for permanent aviaries only. Creepers can be run over the wires. There is nothing better than some of the large-leaved ivy, as it throws off the wet, and is also evergreen, so that the aviary looks well all the year round.

Perches are best made out of deal quartering, 2in. by 2in., with the edges run off; this does not split. Oak and ash poles split, and the birds lose their claws in them. Pheasants generally select the highest perch to roost on, but they prefer a very wide board or cill —probably it is less fatiguing than a perch. Between the aviaries have doors rising and falling in grooves, such as is usual in fowl-houses. These you should be able to raise with a string outside, and, if you have one empty aviary, you can in turn change all your birds, and clean all the aviaries without disturbing them. This is a decided advantage. You may plant shrubs if you like, but then, of course, you cannot have concrete floors. There must be plenty of dry, fine sand in a corner for the dust-bath, and old mortar where the birds lay.

Nothing tends more to the healthfulness of the birds than changing their aviaries and cleaning them out, well raking the surface, and adding a little fine gravel or coarse sand. If your floors are not of concrete, you must dig them up roughly, add a little lime, and let the aviaries lie empty awhile.

Erect as many aviaries as you require, all in a row, and let them face south-east to south, if possible.

Do not fear that the birds will die of exposure. I have had 5ft. of snow in the aviaries, and the thermometer 3° below zero, and never lost a bird. Most of my pheasants come from cold countries, and

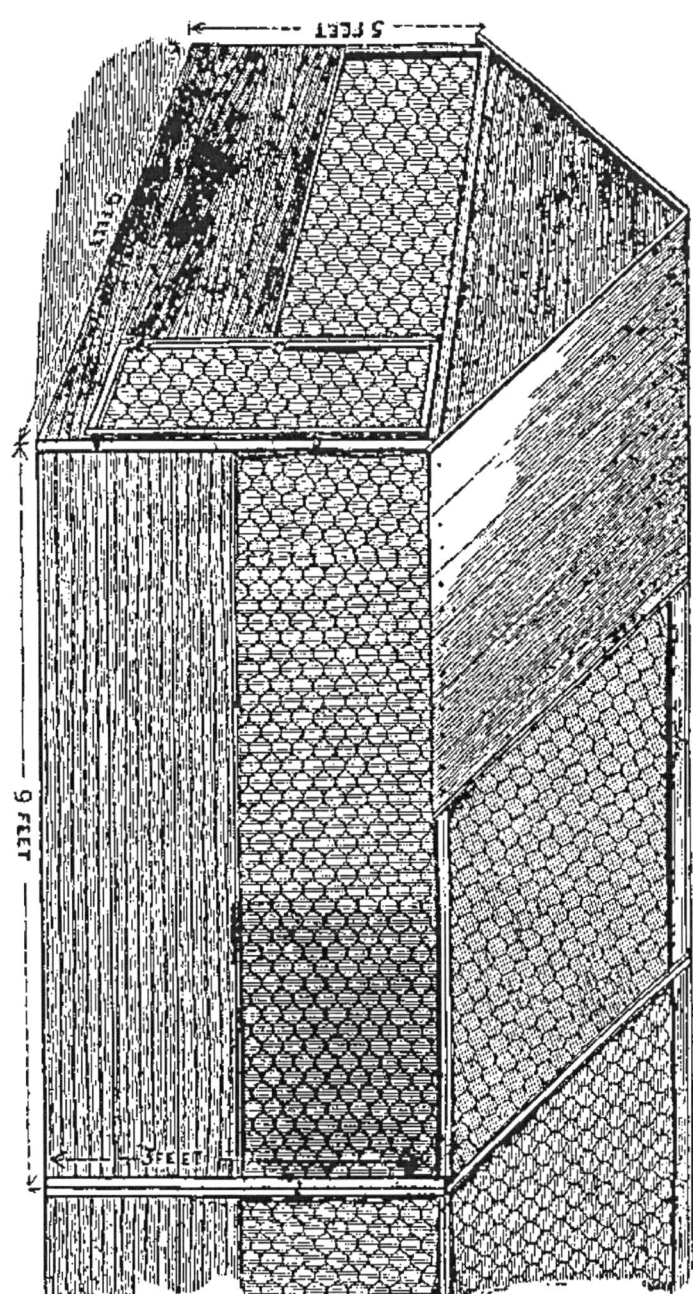

FIG. 2.—PORTABLE AVIARY.

are very hardy. I have twenty Gold cocks in one aviary in a very exposed position, and with little or no shelter, and often find them with snow and frost on their backs, but they appear none the worse for it. During the winter of 1885-6 many of the birds, when fed early in the morning, were perfectly white with hoar-frost. Do not forget to supply plenty of fresh spring water in these aviaries.

PORTABLE AVIARIES.

These are now made in panels (see Fig. 2). Each panel is 9ft. long and 5ft. high, to form sides, and can be extended to any length. Three lengths are most convenient, or two if only for a cock and five or six hens; one panel forms the end. There is a close roof at each end, formed of boards; the rest is wire netting in panels. The whole takes to pieces, and can be stacked away when not required. It is readily moved by putting a couple of larch poles under it, and using them as rollers, or sliding it sideways on them. The panels and angles are put together with coach screws, the ties form perches, and other perches are 2ft. from the ground, and form lower ties. The following are the scantlings of timbers, &c.: Uprights, 2in. by 1½in. quartering; sides, three 9in. boards, ½in. thick, and one 4½in. board for base, 1in. thick; gable ends, ½in. boards; rafters, 2in. by 1½in. quartering; ridge, 1in. by 4½in. boards; roof, ½in. boards; with fillets over joints.

Frame the rafters together, and notch them to

drop on the plate. This will be found the most convenient aviary possible. I cannot speak too highly of it. It was designed for a special purpose, and costs between £5 and £6.

PORTABLE AVIARIES FOR YOUNG BIRDS.

When the young birds are so large that they will not come in to roost, or when the hen beats them off, they should be placed in a movable aviary, unless you have a large, inclosed place where no cats can get at them, and where the birds cannot get out—in fact, where they are wired in. If this is on grass, with shrubs, &c., nothing could be better. If you have not this convenience, make a portable pen, say, 2ft. high, 6ft. wide, and 9ft. long. Have a sliding trap-door at one end, and closely board all the sides, but wire in the top. It is well to have a shelter at one end.

Move the birds daily on grass if you have it, and, when they are nearly full grown, and you want to remove them to the aviary, put a coop, with food in it, at the trap-door, raise the door, and, when the birds are in the coop, lower the trap. Catch them through the door in the coop. It is well to throw a sack over it and thrust in your arms, or they may slip out. They can then be put where you intend them to remain. Be sure they agree, and that you do not put too many into one inclosure. Do all you can for their comfort, and so keep them in health and growing condition.

The portable runs are very handy in winter to protect lettuces, &c.; or you can make the top in one frame and the four sides the same, and the whole can readily be fastened together with coach screws, and taken apart when not required.

Coops.

The coops I use (A, Fig. 3) were first made some years ago, and are now much improved. They are of good, sound, yellow or red deal, and are made of

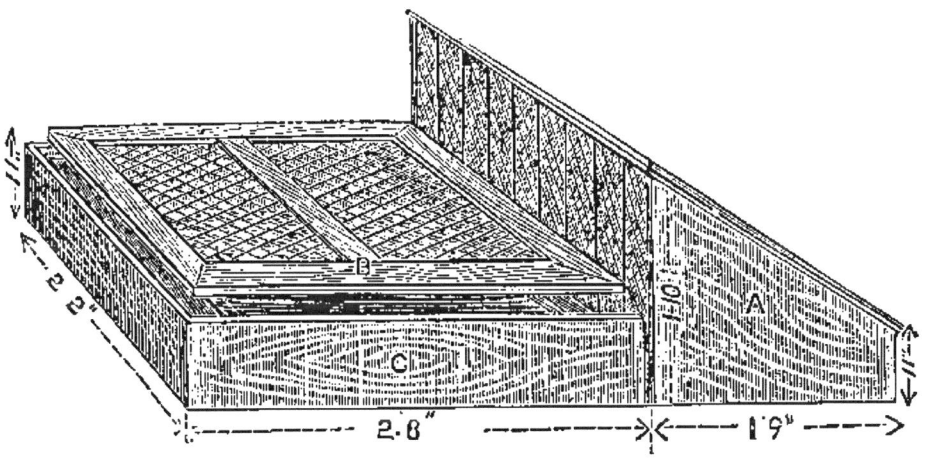

Fig. 3.—Coop and Run.

uniform size, so that the various parts interchange. They have one 11in. board at the back, and are 24in. wide (out to out), 21in. deep (front to back), 22¾in. high in front. The bars are 2in. apart. There is a hole in the roof, 8in. by 9in., with a trap-door (movable), and a button to fasten it down. The sides are best made of one 11in. board at the bottom, and one diagonally cut for the upper part. Thus one board, cross cut, forms part of the two sides, and there is no waste.

The runs or inclosures (C, Fig. 3) are one 11in. board deep, 2ft. 8in. long, and 2ft. wide inside, so as to clip the sides of the coop. Just within the top of this run fits a frame (B), made of strips 2ft. 6in. long, or 2in. shorter than the run, and having cross strips 1in. thick and 3in. wide; to this 1in. mesh galvanised netting is fastened with $\frac{3}{4}$in. staples. The frame is supported by falling on strips, which help to keep the run together, and, when in its place, is flush with the top; no cat can scratch it out. Fig. 3 will show all this plainly. The material is $\frac{3}{4}$in. thick, and should be really sound, good stuff. The coops cost about 7s. 6d. each to make, and, with a coat of paint each spring, and scrubbing after use, will last for years. To the front of each coop fasten a piece of netting, similar to that on the runs, placing the selvedge downwards. A piece of netting, 2ft. wide, divided down the middle, will suffice for two, and when the run is closed at night it will be perfectly vermin-proof. All the coops and inclosures being uniform, much trouble is saved. The door in the roof is better than the old-fashioned sliding bar in front. Put a screw top and bottom into one of the bars; this will enable you readily to remove the bar if you wish to set a hen in the coop. To shut her off, drop down one of the boards that go under the coop (described below).

To each coop there are two bottom boards, thus keeping the hen dry. One of the boards is placed under the coop, and the other, each night, or in driving rain, leans against the roof of the coop, and is sloped on to the run; this prevents the birds getting wet. They are made of ½in. stuff, exactly as wide as the coop, but of three 9in. boards, nailed so that they are 27in. by 24in. The little trap-door in the roof of the coop is supported on two slips, and the button on the coop prevents the hen getting out if so disposed. At night an old sack is put over the coop, and about 1ft. of it hangs over the front; this is turned back during the day. The soiled bottom board is changed each day.

The best way to change the soiled board is to place a clean one behind it, and, when the birds are out, slide hen and coop on to the latter, taking up the dirty one, and placing the run in the proper position; thus they are easily shifted on to fresh ground. After a fortnight or so, they will not require bottom boards, unless the weather is wet.

CHAPTER III.

BREEDING.

When to Obtain Stock—Persecution of Hens by Cocks: How to Prevent—Early Layers—Laying Hens—Shelters—Dangers of Laying in the Open—Feeding—Setting—Treatment of Sitting Hens—Making a Nest—Soiling from Broken Eggs—Sitting Boxes: Ventilation of—Damping Eggs—Testing Eggs—Hatching—Chipped Eggs—Christy's Egg Protector—Incubators: Advantages of.

IT is certainly best to obtain your stock and young birds in the autumn; they get more used to the place, tamer, and, in every way, settle down better, than old birds. Under the several varieties, I shall indicate the requisite number of hens to be kept to each cock. In all varieties, the cock will sometimes persecute the hen, plucking her head bare and picking out her eyes. The best plan to avoid this is to cut one of his wings hard; this will allow her to escape him. Still, if he is determined, it will go hard with her, and she must be removed. Amhersts are terrible tyrants—some cocks kill every hen; but, during the winter months, you may keep many cocks together, without much danger, if there are no hens with them. Most varieties lay early in the spring. The Elliot is the earliest as far as my experience goes; mine laid on 16th March, 1885, in deep snow.

Laying Hens.—The very first thing to be observed is to disturb and worry the laying birds as little as possible. If they are timid and shy, always wear the same dress when you visit them; and, especially when entering the aviaries to collect eggs, do not talk loudly, or allow strangers to bring in dogs or to poke at the birds with sticks; be as gentle and quiet as possible. The aviaries should be kept clean, the water fresh and good (spring), with a little iron tonic (Douglas' mixture) used in it at least once each week, and the birds supplied with abundance of green food; the best, by far, is lettuce, but they will eat watercress, chickweed, cabbage leaves, and broccoli. Do not over-feed, or the birds will produce soft eggs. The bottom of the pens should be clear of large, rough stones; it is best to have sand over fine gravel.

Supposing, now, that you have birds commencing to lay, you will probably have formed some hiding-place in a corner for them. I have used bushes, faggots, natural shrubs, and all sorts of devices, but, in spite of everything, I find the hens lay in the open as often as under cover. A good shelter can be formed by nailing two 11in. boards on to strips of wood, 36in. long, one board just meeting or overlapping the other. The boards may run the whole width of the aviary, or along the north side if possible; they should be placed sloping against the building, leaving, say, 9in. open on the lower side, the ends of strips entering the ground, thus forming a good lean-to. Under this the birds are sure to lay, and also to dust themselves.

Unfortunately, the danger of the birds laying in the open is that they may accidentally break their eggs; this invariably leads to egg-eating, and then all hopes of breeding are at an end, for, watch as you may, you are sure to lose a great many. The cock is generally the culprit, and the hens soon acquire the habit. There are many plans to cure this habit. Sham eggs I have not found of any service; the birds know them, and do not attempt to break them after the first trial; but no sooner is an egg laid than it is broken. Some persons pare down the point of the upper bill, so that it may be soft; I have tried this, but cannot say I have met with invariable success. Others slightly touch the beak with a hot poker, so as to burn the extreme point, and I really think that is the best, and has proved the most successful, method. Another plan is to put mustard into an egg-shell; but that is of no use whatever—the birds are found to eat it greedily, even with paraffin added to it. The only remaining plan I know, is using the eggs of common fowls, and letting the birds eat their fill. Some varieties, certainly, are greater delinquents than others: Reeves' are very troublesome, but Versicolors never do it. No doubt the habit is acquired, in the first instance, from eating broken eggs. I have known birds to regularly eat their eggs one year, and not to do so the following season; yet one can hardly suppose they have forgotten the habit.

The birds should be regularly fed; all will depend on this. Feed early in the morning, and again towards evening; use barley, wheat, rice, and very little maize, for it produces too much internal fat. At times give a little Chamberlin's Food. I do not say other foods are not as good, but I have used this for nearly twenty years. Add Spratts Crissel in small quantities. Put old mortar, cinders (of which the birds are very fond), sharp grit, or small gravel, in the pens, and take care there is a dry dusting-place—pheasants like to roll in the dust and bask in the sun. Occasionally rake the aviary over, if the birds are not alarmed by your doing so; or, if the next pen is empty, and you can let them run through into that, they will enjoy the fresh surface, and be undoubtedly the better for it. The birds are very fond of freshly-cut lawn mowings and other grass.

When the eggs are collected, put them in fresh, sweet bran, small end downwards; let them be turned every day, but the less time they are kept before setting the better. When you have enough eggs, prepare to set them; you should, before this, have provided a quiet, light hen—the best by far, for these small pheasants are the cross produced between a silky cock and a game hen or game bantam. Pure silkies are very good, but they are apt to have scaly legs.

The cross mentioned above is of a fair size, yet light, and keeps a long time with the young birds. It entirely depends on the variety of eggs how many you should set; if a large sort, like Reeves', select a larger hen than for small, like the Gold. Under her put from eleven to thirteen eggs. I dislike large broods; the small hens cannot cover them when they get any size, and you have much trouble to count them at night when you shut them in. Therefore, select the hens and eggs proportionately to each other.

During the laying season, it is well at times to supply fresh gravel, old mortar, or ashes; the birds must have material of which to make the shells. Put a little iron tonic (Douglas' mixture) in the water once a week, and be sure the birds are well supplied with clean, hard water. By gentle treatment, and feeding with little delicacies (such as lettuce or a few hemp seeds), they will learn to eat from the hand; this tameness adds greatly to the pleasure of keeping birds. Wild birds dashing themselves against the wires run great risk of being killed, in addition to spoiling their plumage.

Treatment of Sitting Hens.—You will always find a fowl that steals her nest do better than one you set, because she strictly follows Nature; we must, therefore, follow Nature as closely as possible if we wish for success. You can set the hen either in a sitting-box (Figs. 4 and 5), or in a bottomless box, having three sides high, and the fourth low, so that the hen may conveniently enter or leave it. The box should be placed in one of the ordinary coops, taking care that one of its bars is movable, either by unscrewing or by raising; I prefer the former method. The run must be placed in front, and may be made of any convenient size, so that the hen can feed and dust herself. Any wire or wood inclosure that will fit up

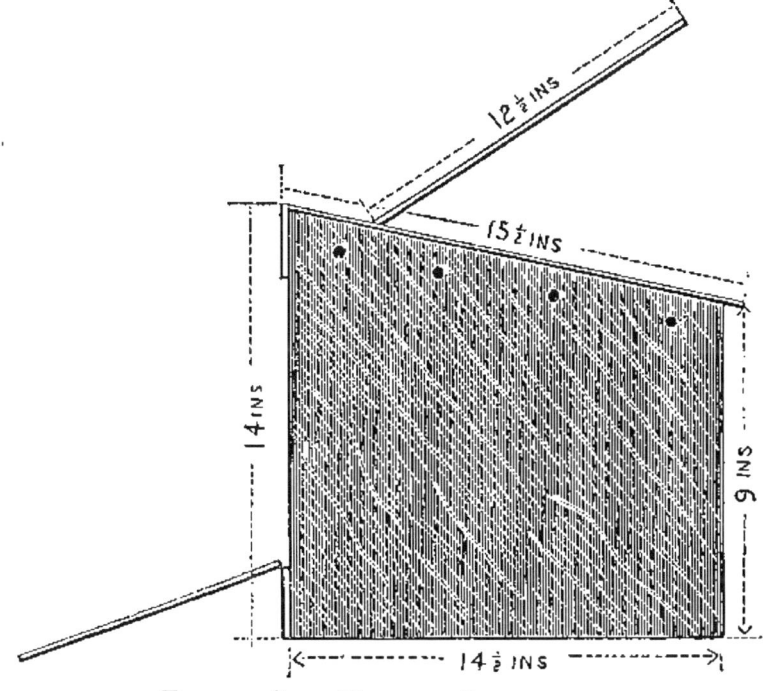

FIG. 4.—SIDE VIEW OF SITTING-BOX.

to the coop will answer the purpose. The hen may be removed through a hole in the roof of the coop. She can be taken off, and fed in the run; on withdrawing the bar, at the end of fifteen to twenty minutes, she will speedily return to the nest. In very large establishments, like the Maharajah Dhuleep

Singh's game farm at Elvedon, wire runs with sitting-boxes at the sides are used; the hens are turned off the nests, and put into wire runs, very similar to those described under "Coops," in Chapter II.

Whichever way you adopt, you first make a nest by placing a turf, grass downwards, and hollow in the centre, in the middle of the box. See that it is nice and hollow—with no hard knobs or stones—place in it two or three sham eggs, and put the hen on them the last thing at night. Take her off next morning, at the hour at which you intend for the future to feed her. When she has taken food and water, restore her to her nest, and, if she settles down well, you may, in the course of the day, put the eggs under her. Enter the particulars in the "Sitting-hen Record,"* and affix the second half of the label to her coop. If you have used a sitting-box without a run or inclosure, you can put a tether with a slip-knot round the hen's leg. Take a slip of leather a few inches long, cut a slit at one end, and put the other end through it; to this fasten a string, and, with a good length of it, fix her to a peg. Pass her leg through the leather loop, and she will be quite secure. The keepers usually peg the sitting hens on a piece of turf at equal distances from each other, forming a square, and pans of water and food are placed within reach —a plan I do not much like.

You might put the hen in an empty coop, with

---

* Published by L. Upcott Gill, 170, Strand, London. Price, 50 Forms, 6d.; 100 Forms, 1s.

food and water in front; she can dust herself in this coop, and, when the time is up, you can catch her, lower the front flap of the sitting-box (Fig. 5) and place her near it, and she will go in by herself. If an egg gets broken, or bursts, when you have removed the hen for feeding, cleanse the nest, wash the other eggs in warm water, and see that the hen has no mess on her breast, or it will stick to the eggs, and cause further damage. The best plan is to cut off the soiled feathers with a pair of scissors; at all

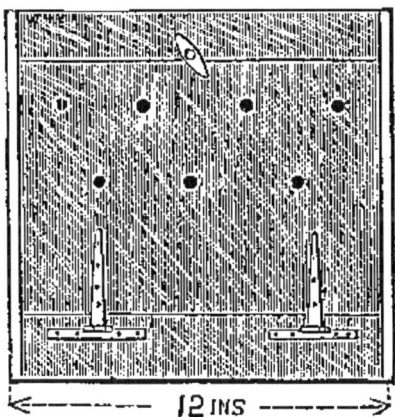

FIG. 5.—FRONT VIEW OF SITTING-BOX.

events, be sure she is perfectly clean. If she has had a good dust-bath, that will have cleansed her.

All sitting-boxes should have plenty of ventilation; the building, or whatever place they are in, should be kept cool, sweet, and clean. It is well to place a little short hay or dry grass beneath the eggs. There is a question as to the length of time it is desirable for the hen to be off her eggs. This much depends on the weather; if very cold, the small eggs of pheasants will cool quickly; but I have known a hen on Amherst eggs accidentally shut off her nest for upwards of an hour, and they hatched well. Undoubtedly, the nearer they are to hatching, the longer time the hen may be off the eggs, for it will take a long chill to destroy life when near hatching. I do not like nests placed tier over tier; they are best on the ground. After the first week, damp the eggs when the hens have returned. Dipping a sponge in

FIG. 6.—TESTING EGGS.

warm water, and gently passing it over them, is a good plan. This causes a nice damp heat to rise, and is preferable to sprinkling, unless the weather is very hot. Damping the eggs when the hen is on them seems most natural, and in effect is like the damp breast of the mother, which in Nature has become moistened with dew in her search for food. Each morning, at the same time, remove the hens for feeding, dusting themselves, &c.

Many keepers test the eggs for fertility after they have been under the hen a week or ten days; I seldom do so—the less they are disturbed the better. If they are to be tested, take a stout piece of card or millboard, about 9in. square, colour one side black, and in the centre cut an egg-shaped hole rather smaller than the eggs to be examined. The edge of the hole should be slightly bevelled. Then take the eggs, board, and a bright lamp, into a dark room; hold the board in front of the lamp, and place an egg in the hole, holding them as close to the flame of the lamp as possible (see Fig. 6). If the eggs are fertile, they will appear dark; but if unfertile, they will be translucent. It is better to remove the globe of the lamp, as you want the light concentrated as much as possible.

Hatching.—Eggs are due to hatch on the twenty-second or twenty-fourth day; the Gold will sometimes hatch in twenty-one days. If you find an egg chipped, and it has not advanced after an interval of, say, eight hours, place it for a minute or two in a basin of warm water (blood heat)— not deep, or it will drown the chicken—the damaged part uppermost. This softens the membrane, and quickly assists hatching. Take care not to draw the chicken from the shell, or you may do so before the yolk is absorbed, and that will be fatal. If you find the shell coming off, leaving the membrane-like parchment, and the egg in danger of being crushed by a heavy hen, put the egg in a Christy's egg-protector

(Fig. 7); I have used them for some years, and have even put two partridges' or quails' eggs in one, and saved the two. They are little brass "egg-shells," rather larger than the eggs, and are made in two sizes, to take fowls' or pheasants' eggs. When you cannot get the bird to come out, you may, with a straw bent at an angle, enlarge the hole, or slightly crack the shell in a line with the first opening. All this requires the greatest care, or you will make the chick bleed, and then the hopes of saving it are but slight. When the chicks

FIG. 7.—CHRISTY'S EGG-PROTECTOR.

are out, they should be left undisturbed for twelve hours; they get dry and strong, and do not require food. You may place a little food close to the hen if you find any of the chicks disposed to run out, and she will teach them to eat. Take care they do not stray, as they do not yet know her call. Undoubtedly, the less the hens are disturbed the better, and perhaps we lose more than we save by disturbing them and rendering them restless; much depends on the temperament of the hen.

Some persons prefer to place the egg, when near hatching, in an incubator; this was the system adopted at the Maharajah's; the incubator was not one of those used entirely for hatching. The chipped eggs are placed in the incubator to avoid the risk of crushing by big hens, and when they are hatched the young are placed in the "mother," which forms the upper portion. Here they get strong and dry, learn to feed, creep under the flannel, and become quite at home; meanwhile, one or two eggs have been left with the hen, and when all are hatched they are removed to the ground where they are to be reared. I turn them into a kitchen garden, because I find there so much food for the young birds, and there is less chance of their straying away. If you cannot do this, a well-kept lawn or level meadow, or, better still, an orchard, will answer the purpose. I strongly advise that it be wired in. The coops are better placed a day or two before required, so as to keep the ground dry; in fact, it is best to arrange all just as if the birds were in them. The next thing is—when all are hatched, dry, and well—to put the chicks out; a south-east or south aspect is the best. If any are weakly, they must be kept in the incubator or house till fit to put out. By putting them under the hen late at night, they have less chance of being noticed by her.

CHAPTER IV.

REARING.

First Treatment—Feeding—After-treatment—Treatment of Diarrhœa—Cutting the Wings of Young Birds.

HAVING now described the laying, sitting, and hatching, I must treat on putting out the young birds and hen. I find it a good plan to remove the hen, for a few minutes, to a spare coop; give her food and water, and try to get her to eat. By this plan she does not soil the clean coop. In a short time, place her gently in the one she is to occupy, and give her the chicks. At first they do not understand her call; but if you give her a little of their food, she will be sure to call them, and you must endeavour to confine them to their coop for the first few hours. You can do this with a bottom board. They will not require water at first. After a short time, give pure spring water in a clean saucer full of stones as large as walnuts; this prevents the chickens getting in and having cramp.

Never stint clean water; yet, at first, remove it after they have drunk.

Do not place the coops too close together, unless the hens are very friendly to each other's chicks, or they will kill the young ones. Some hens seem to attract any number of chicks to them; others kill all strange birds. Select such a situation as will leave the birds little disturbed by visitors, dogs, &c. Should the weather be very hot and dry, water the sack that is thrown over the coop. I take it for granted that the coop is placed on a path, if in the garden, or at the side of a lawn; it certainly is better there than on grass. The footpaths must, each year, be well cleaned, dug up, and lime and fresh gravel added, so that the birds are really on fresh ground. The borders being also dug, the whole gives variety to birds reared year after year on exactly the same spot.

Feeding.—The next matter is the food; and this is most important. Never use hard-boiled eggs; they are the most indigestible stuff possible, and dry in the sun like flints. Custard is the food at first; make it of eggs and milk, nice and dry; to it add a few crushed hemp seeds, and chopped lettuce and onion tops; the little fellows will soon peck at the onion tops. Place a turf in the middle of the run about the second day, and put a little food on it; the chicks delight in searching for it. About the third or fourth day, quietly draw back the run about 2in.; presently, one of the little birds will slip out, and soon run in again; then they will go longer distances, but they must not be allowed to go far till they know the hen's call, or they will be lost. As they get older, diminish the custard, and use Chamberlin's Food, with Spratts Crissel added. The following is what I rear chicks on: Rice well boiled (not sticky), chopped onions and their tops, crushed hemp, a little pepper, and instead of Chamberlin's Food, baked breadcrumbs, well ground. Sprinkle the food with a little iron tonic, and let the whole be mixed till quite dry. Never let it get sour, or be left from day to day: only put enough the last thing at night for the early breakfast. Do not forget, the younger the birds, the more custard. They will soon learn to eat grits and unboiled rice; they are very fond of ants' eggs, but, unless the supply can be kept up, it should not be begun. Let them have plenty of fresh lettuce; tear the leaves into pieces. For the hen, put her food in one corner of the coop, or she will eat all theirs if she can get at it.

Feed little and often, and very early. Of course, as the young ones get older they will not require stones in the water. To confine them to their coop during, say, the first twenty-four hours, you may either use one of the bottom boards (only that makes it dark inside) or an 11in. board; the run will keep it in position. The chicks are apt to stray into the run in the early morning, and get cramp, if not shut in at night till nearly a week old. You may use a miniature cucumber frame, the size of the run, and made like it, except the glass slopes. Being on hinges, and of the same height as the coop, in very stormy weather it proves useful for the first few days; and during sunshine it is pleasant and warm to the young birds.

After-Treatment.—When the birds are getting strong, and running everywhere, be regular in your feeding times as well as at first, so that they know when to expect it. Feed just before shutting-up time. Count the birds, and push the run to the coop. When they are all in, turn down the sack, place the sloping bottom board to keep off the rain, and they are safe till, say, five o'clock the next morning. Let the hen have a little of the young birds' food; it induces her to call them. When they run out regularly, they will eat every bit of lettuce and onion they can reach, and will forage amongst the vegetable beds. Your gardener may not like them in the garden, but, for getting birds on, there is no place like it. They run out and feed, then scamper back under the hen, and will beat any birds in a state of nature where the mother drags them about through wet grass and all sorts of places. If they do eat some vegetables, they, in return, clear the garden of insects, &c., and to their own manifest advantage.

Should you find any birds disposed to diarrhœa, clip the feathers round the vent, and wash it clean; otherwise, it is apt to clog, and the bird becomes miserable, and soon dies.

Cutting the Wings of Young Birds—If you let your birds loose in a garden, or wired inclosure, unless it is covered in at the top they will, in a short time, be able to fly and escape: this is easily prevented by cutting one wing. The operation is not so easy as it appears, for, no sooner do you try to catch the birds, than the mothers become excited, jump about, and will probably stand on some of the little ones, and break their legs or backs. The best plan is, when the little ones are having their first feed in the morning, to take out the hen through the trap-door of the

Fig. 8.—Cutting the Wing of a Pheasant.

coop, and then, when the chicks miss her, to put food inside the coop, and entice them there. Quickly drop down one of the bottom boards, and you will have them all safe inside. Put in your arm while the sack is round the coop, or they will be sure to slip out, and remove them one at a time. Hold each bird in the hollow of the left hand (see Fig. 8), with its breast downwards, head towards you; get its legs under the little finger, and then cut close the long or flight feathers of the wing—mind you do not cut the legs. Turn the bird down close to the coop; and so in turn proceed with all. Now restore the hen to her coop, remove the bottom board, open the run, and she will entice the chicks back to her. After a time, you will require to cut the other wing, for the one cut will speedily grow, and it is best to cut them in turn.

When going to roost, or if suddenly alarmed, there is great danger of their flying, for, after a while, they will get very troublesome, and unwilling to come in at night, especially if the weather be hot. There would be no harm in their remaining outside if it were not for the risk of cats. If the plan is suitable, a run extending at the back of the aviaries, having a trap-door into each, would be found most serviceable. You could, by means of this, pass the birds from one aviary to another, say, three or four or more off, and you might rear the half-grown birds in it, and also pass them direct into the permanent aviaries.

CHAPTER V.

THE GOLD PHEASANT
(*Thaumalea picta*).

Introduction—A Universal Favourite—Value of its Plumage to the Fisherman—Colours of Cock—Colours of Hen—Distinguishing Characteristics of Male and Female—Advantages as Pets—Vices—Grace in Movement and Splendid Plumage—Breeding—Number of Hens to a Cock.

OF all our aviary pheasants, the Gold, first brought to Europe, it is said, in the fifteenth century, is most probably the best known and greatest favourite. Its brilliant plumage and restless disposition—ever on the move, except for the short time when it is moulting, and when it seems to be very subdued and quiet—cause this bird to be universally admired. To these qualities must be added the value of its plumage to the salmon fisherman. Nearly all the feathers are of value: in the crest, or topping, every feather is of use; next come the collar or tippet, the red breast feather, yellow saddle, the spear or red outside feather

GOLD AND SILVER PHEASANTS
(*Thaumalea picta* and *Euplocamus nycthemerus*).

at the base of the tail, and the two centre feathers of the tail—all sought after. Good, rich, deep-coloured toppings will always command a price; but soiled, shed, or moulted feathers are of no value.

The adult cock has his crest varying from pale straw to almost deep orange. This latter colour has of late years become very prevalent, but it is not correct; it has been caused by the introduction of Amherst blood; the right colour is very pale orange. The longer the crest, the more valuable the bird. The tippet should be of deep orange, margined with blue-black, with another similar bar a short distance above; breast deep, rich red; shoulder dark green; wing coverts steel-blue; tail brown, with round, black spots, and about five spear or stiff red feathers on each side. The hen is of a quiet brown; feathers having black margins, and more yellow than the hen of the Amherst. Both sexes should have yellow legs. Eye of male, white; of hen, brown. For the first year, the sexes are nearly alike, but are readily distinguished by the eye of the cock, and by signs of coming crest feathers.

Of all the pheasants for pets, probably none is so suitable as the Gold; it is not large like the Reeves' or the Silvers. It requires but little room, is very hardy, easy to rear, readily tamed, and always in demand if you wish to sell. Like everything else, however, it has its drawbacks: it does not come into full plumage until a year old, and the cock is very pugnacious and apt to kill the hens, as does also its congener, the Lady Amherst. But its graceful movements always charm the human beholder. I have constantly had over twenty adult males in one aviary; and when in full spring plumage, and on a bright day, incessantly dancing about, they are truly a splendid sight to a bird-lover.

It has been stated that the young do not breed the first year. I have hatched eleven eggs out of thirteen, and repeatedly proved this statement to be an error; yet I am not sure it was not correct when these birds were first bred in England. The same was said of the Amherst, and I did not get their young birds to breed at first, but now I do in some instances. I think an adult cock with a young hen is always fertile; but, as a rule, I believe birds do not breed until they are in full plumage. You may keep two or even three hens to a cock.

CHAPTER VI.

THE SILVER PHEASANT
(Euplocamus nycthemerus).

Introduction — Points Recommended for — Colours of Cock — Colours of Hen — Number of Hens to Cock — Pugnacity of Cocks — Domesticity — Feeding.

PROBABLY the Silver Pheasant (said to have been introduced into Europe about 1600, from the South of China) is better known in aviaries than any other variety except the Gold. It is certainly a handsome bird, hardy, a free breeder, and one that soon becomes very tame. It does not obtain full plumage till the second year.

The adult male has a black crest, the face being covered with brilliant red wattles (when excited, these are erected), the throat and under part of the body steel-black; upper portion of body white, delicately marked with black lines, the wing-coverts being well margined with black; centre tail feathers white, the others shaded with black; legs red. The hen is not so large as the cock, and is of a dull brown, with tracings of black.

One hen is generally kept to each cock. The adult cocks are frequently extremely pugnacious, and will attack anyone entering their aviary. I have seen one repeatedly fly at his feeder, and spur his legs; in one instance, the man tried to beat the cock with his cap, and the bird split the cap open with its spur. Silvers are easily brought up to feed with the fowls, and I have known them perfectly tame in a farmyard, feeding with the poultry. The Silver pheasant is a very long-lived bird in captivity. It is useless as a sporting bird, and I never knew anyone to eat it. Silvers are, probably, the least valuable of any aviary pheasants.

Feed the young exactly as you do the young of other pheasants; they are very hardy, and, with ordinary attention, will present no difficulties in rearing.

LADY AMHERST PHEASANTS
(*Thaumalea Amherstiæ*).

CHAPTER VII.

THE LADY AMHERST PHEASANT
(*Thaumalea Amherstiæ*).

Introduction—Suitability for Rearing in a Wild State —Uses to the Salmon-fly Maker—Colours of Cock —Colours of Hen—Breeding and Rearing—Quarrelsome Cocks and Hens—Number of Hens to Cock —Hardiness—Feeding.

THE first of these birds were brought to this country by Lady Amherst. They soon died, and it was left to Mr. Stone, of Scyborwen, near Monmouth, in 1869, to be the introducer of the stock from which our first birds were bred; since that time many have been imported, and the birds are now very general favourites. At first the prices were very high, but they are now moderate enough to place the birds within the reach of most pheasant-keepers. Amhersts do well even in a wild state; and a great many, and also their crosses with the Gold, are now at large in the Earl of Annesley's grounds, at Castlewellan, Co. Down. Lord Tweedmouth has also written to me that he has had a cock at liberty for some time on his estate in Inverness-shire. I think for aviary purposes the Amherst is the handsomest of the genus, as distinguished from true pheasants (*Phasianus*), and the best for fanciers with a limited space.

The Amherst cock is a graceful and elegant bird. Although his feathers are not so valuable as those of the Gold, some are very useful to the salmon-fly maker. The bird is larger than the Gold; crest black, with a few red feathers, the whole crest being much shorter than that of the Gold; iris white; face pale green; tippet white, edged and barred with green and black like that of the Gold; breast deep green, edged with black; back, ditto; belly white; saddle orange-red; tail, two centre feathers of great length, grey with black bars, laced, outer feathers grey, shaded with brown, and having semicircular bars of black; inner web black and white mottled; legs lead colour. The hens are very similar to the Gold, but with a rich chestnut head, and altogether of a richer brown, but not so yellow on the breast.

Probably I have bred more Amhersts than anyone else in England, and I find they require no special care. They do not obtain their full plumage till the second year, and it was said they did not breed till that age; but this is incorrect. These birds were at first supposed to require a warm aviary, but I have had mine roost in the open, in the winter of 1880-81, with the thermometer 3° below zero, and 5ft. of driven snow in their aviaries, and I think they rather enjoyed it. They do not like wet or damp weather—

in fact, no pheasants do, and those with long tails look very wretched.

The hens are quarrelsome amongst themselves. You may keep two hens to each cock for breeding. Be sure the cock agrees with the hens, for some cocks are regular Bluebeards, and kill every hen, and that very quickly, picking out their eyes and scalping them.

Amhersts are decidedly hardy when young, and have no special diseases. Give plenty of chopped onion and lettuce; let the food be as directed in Chapter IV.; keep clean, and supply clean water; and, if bred from healthy stock, you will rear one of the best varieties of aviary pheasants. I have not found hemp seed injure these birds, as it certainly does the Reeves'.

CHAPTER VIII.

THE SWINHOE PHEASANT
(*Euplocamus Swinhœi*).

Introduction—Treatment—Colours of Cock—Colours of Hen—Number of Hens to Cock—Domesticity.

OF the same genus as the Silver, but, I think, much handsomer, is the Swinhoe pheasant. These birds are not so large, but the colours of the male are very beautiful. Their habits are similar to, and they require the same treatment as, the Silver. The variety was introduced to Europe, from Formosa, about 1863.

The adult male has a pure white crest, and red wattles, which, when excited, he erects till they meet in a point on the top of his head, and present a very singular appearance. The under side of the body is deep steel-blue, back of head ditto, lower part of neck white, shoulders maroon, wing brilliant green; the longest feathers black, edged with green; saddle steel-blue; centre tail feathers white, lyre-shaped; lower ones blue-black; legs brilliant red. The hen is very similar to the Silver hen, but rather lighter, and with pointed breast feathers.

The hen lays from eight to ten eggs. The young do not obtain their full plumage till the second year; in some instances they breed the first year. Keep one hen to a cock.

Swinhoes do not make much progress with admirers of pheasants. There is nothing specially attractive in their habits, and they appear to be far from favourites; yet they are pretty, very easily tamed, and should not be absent from the collection of *Euplocami*.

In the hope that these birds may attract more attention than they have hitherto done, and to which their beauty, and the ease with which they are managed, entitle them, I have given a coloured plate of them as a frontispiece.

CHAPTER IX.

THE SŒMMERRING PHEASANT
(Phasianus Sæmmerringii).

Introduction—Precautions to Protect Hens from Cocks —Colours of Cock—Colours of Hen—Domesticity— Number of Hens to Cock—P. Scintillans.

MR. REGINALD RUSSELL is said to have introduced this variety, in 1864. At present there are but few specimens in this country, for, unfortunately, the males are most pugnacious, and very apt to kill the females. The best precaution that we know of is to cut one wing hard, and to leave plenty of cover to conceal the hen.

The adult male is very handsome—a golden copper colour, every feather having a margin of white and black; eye red; tail also reddish, with wide, reddish bars, shading into a pale colour. The bird is called Ki-ji in Japan, from the note he makes; and, by some, the Copper pheasant. I am told by persons who have shot them, that they look like meteors as they flash in the sun when flying. Those who have seen living specimens, even in this country,

SŒMMERRING'S PHEASANTS

(*Phasianus Sœmmerringii*).

will well understand this, so brilliant is the plumage. The hen has the general colours of the male, but less brilliant; tail, short and round.

A pair of these birds, belonging to a friend of mine, are very tame. The cock fairly drives his feeder out of the aviary, and then struts about as if in defiance. This male has been also mated with a common hen pheasant, but the eggs were not fertile. Sœmmerrings require no special treatment, and I never knew more than one hen kept with a cock.

There is another variety of this species, called *P. scintillans*, but I doubt if it is anything more than a sport, and do not think you could breed them true to colour.

CHAPTER X.

REEVES' PHEASANT
(*Phasianus Reevesii*).

A Noble Bird—Introduction—Large Numbers Bred —Tail: Length, Markings, and Shape—Colours of Cock—Colours of Hen—Adaptability for Breeding and Rearing—Number of Hens to Cock—Pugnacity of Cocks—Eating Eggs—Treatment for Hatching and Rearing—Feeding—" The Pheasant of the Future"—Packing.

UNDOUBTEDLY the noblest of our pheasants, and by far the largest, is the Reeves'; and if his plumage lacks the gorgeous colours of some other varieties, his length of tail and general appearance will compensate for his quieter, but still handsome, colours. These birds were first brought to this country, in 1831, by Mr. John Reeves. They are natives of China, where the long tail feathers are much prized. Reeves' pheasants are now common all over the United Kingdom; in fact, I have sent them to every part, and no doubt large numbers have been bred by others. Lord Tweedmouth has them

REEVES' PHEASANTS

wild on his estate of Guisachan, Inverness-shire; and he most kindly gave me a fine two-year-old cock, which he had shot, and the total length of the bird is only a trifle under 6ft.

The adult cock has the top of the head white, with minute spots of black on most of the feathers. Below this white scalp is a jet-black band; eye red, with a white streak under it; throat white; upper part of neck black; breast black. The back, down to the tail, has every feather pure golden, edged with black; part of the wing coverts have more black on the gold. The tail feathers are very stiff; the two centre feathers are from 51in. to 53in. long in a good specimen; the edges are chestnut, centre of each pale grey, with semicircular bars of black, and with deep chestnut, verging on red, at the point of each black spot; on one feather, now before me, I can count thirty-nine of these crescent bars. The tail is somewhat fan-shaped, the bird being in the habit of expanding it when excited. The hen is a rich brown, of various shades, with a lighter streak of brown under and over the eye. The eggs are of various shades, very similar to those of the common pheasant, but larger.

It would be impossible to speak too highly of these noble birds, and those who have room will find but little trouble in rearing them; and to the game preserver I would say, What could be grander? They breed as easily as our common ones, and their great size and beauty render them most attractive. The more I see of the Reeves', the better I like them.

I am told they are true "rocketers," and excellent sporting birds. Keep three or four hens to a cock.

The cocks are very pugnacious, and, when fighting, spring high in the air; they are also very bold in the aviaries or pens. I have had several which never allowed me to enter unless armed with a good stick, and I have had many battles. These birds are very apt to eat their eggs when in confinement, and it is a good plan to make a retreat, into which the hen can enter, but having the entrance too small for the cock. The Reeves' cover their eggs with grass, &c. They do not crow like our pheasants, but make a singular calling noise and chuckling.

The hens lay about a dozen eggs, sometimes more, and frequently want to sit. You can put other eggs under them (aviaries not being suitable for rearing the young), and they hatch and bring up chickens quite as well as the common barndoor hens. Leave the little ones entirely to the mother—the cocks never kill them. I think, if a suitable place could be had, it would be better to allow these hens to hatch and rear their own eggs. I have proved that most of the birds of the first year breed, but they do not lay many eggs. I purposely kept, last year, a pen of all young birds, as I wished to test this.

Feed exactly as you do the other varieties. The Reeves' grow very fast, and soon obtain their full plumage, so the young birds will require ample nourishment. Be careful not to give too much maize to the old birds, or they will get too fat. The cocks are liable to indigestion, being greedy feeders. Do not forget an ample supply of green food—not much hemp.

Those who have tried breeding with Reeves' pheasants in this country, say they are the "pheasant of the future," and that they are well suited to our coverts. They certainly are truly majestic birds; they breed freely, and their great size and beauty render them an ornament to any estate. What a picture would be a score or so of these great cocks feeding close up to the mansion, as you frequently see the common pheasant do! As they would elicit the admiration of all, one would hardly have the heart to shoot them. In coverts, these birds keep pretty much to themselves, and, if there are plenty of hens, will not cross with the common pheasant. I hope to see greater efforts made to introduce them, as the price is now very moderate. One hen I bred in 1885 laid thirty eggs the next year.

In packing these birds, ample room must be allowed for the cock's tail; in fact, he is best put in a basket by himself, and the hens in another.

CHAPTER XI.

THE SIAMESE FIREBACK PHEASANT
(Euplocamus prelatus).

Introduction—Unsuitability for Keeping in Confinement—Colours of Cock—Colours of Hen—Conditions necessary for Keeping—Shyness and Restlessness.

THE Siamese Firebacks are natives of Siam, and were first brought to Europe in 1862. I have not heard of any specimens being bred in this country. I tried them, but found them very shy, and but ill-adapted to the confinement of an aviary.

The adult cock has a plume of feathers on his head, which he erects at pleasure. Back of head black; face brilliant red, like the Silver; neck, breast, and shoulders, light grey; wings ditto, with black tracings; saddle yellow, shading into brilliant red and orange; tail steel-blue; legs red. The hen is brown, of the prevailing colour of the other *Euplocami*.

Siamese Firebacks should be kept in pairs. If anyone wishes to try them, large, well-sheltered aviaries, with plenty of evergreens for shelter, should be provided; in these, perhaps, they may breed.

SIAMESE FIREBACK PHEASANTS
(*Euplocamus prelatus*).

Little or nothing is known of this variety in England. After considerable trouble, I imported a pair, but had no success with them; they remained shy and restless to the last. I much doubt there being three pairs of them in Europe.

CHAPTER XII.

THE ELLIOT PHEASANT

(*Gallophasis Ellioti*).

Introduction — Colours of Cock — Colours of Hen — Number of Hens to Cock — Feeding — Rarity — Hatching and Rearing — Hardiness.

IN general appearance this bird is very like the common pheasant, though rather smaller. It is an inhabitant of Upper Thibet, and was first brought to Europe by Mr. Jamrach, in 1879.

In the cock, the crown of the head is greyish-black, with a grey streak over the eye, red wattles, black throat, and white in the lower portion; back of neck grey; breast and shoulders copper, with black marks; a bridle on the back, of pure white; lower part of back and saddle grey, every feather edged with black; wing coverts rufous, with white bars; sides white, with large, black markings; belly white; tail feathers long, grey, with lateral bars of chestnut. The bird, when excited, spreads his tail like a fan. The hen is very similar to the hen of the Reeves' except in having a

ELLIOT'S PHEASANTS
(*Gallophasis Elliotti*).

black patch on the throat, and a round tail, with the outer feathers cinnamon-colour. I am the fortunate possessor of several Elliots. I keep them in pairs, but do not see why three or four hens may not be kept to a cock. Feed exactly as you do the other varieties.

At present, these beautiful birds are rare, and very expensive. They only lay eight or nine eggs. One of my hens wishing to sit, I placed bantam eggs under her, and she has hatched and reared them, and is an excellent mother. It is impossible to say at present what will be the future of these birds in this country, but I feel sure they are hardy enough to stand the climate well; and if they can be bred in sufficient numbers, they will be rare flyers in our coverts, as they are fine sporting birds in appearance, and very swift. They are remarkably neat, clean-built, handsome birds.

CHAPTER XIII.

THE VERSICOLOR OR JAPANESE PHEASANT

(*Phasianus versicolor*).

Introduction—Abundant Layers—Colours of Cock—Colours of Hen—Feeding—Pugnacity of Cocks—Cutting Wings—Number of Hens to Cock—Crossing with the Common Pheasant.

AS the name implies, these birds are natives of Japan, and have been known in Europe about forty-seven years, the first specimens having been brought to Amsterdam. Since our increased intercourse with Japan, considerable quantities have been imported. Versicolors are much smaller than our birds, but I am informed that, when crossed with them, the half-bred birds are of good size. I have not tested this, as I am very particular in keeping only pure blood. The hens are most abundant layers, frequently yielding as many as forty eggs; they are hardy, good eating, and the cross is said to be very desirable in the coverts.

VERSICOLOR, OR JAPANESE PHEASANTS
(*Phasianus versicolor*).

Versicolors are exquisitely beautiful, and yet they have not a single gaudy colour. The cock flaps his wings like the common cock; his crow is very similar, only rather hoarser. He has a deep rifle-green head; wattles red, with minute black feathers all over them; his horns are longer in proportion than those of the common pheasant. The colours of the head shade off on the neck into metallic blue and green; back glaucous-grey; shoulder markings like those of the common pheasant; under part of throat and breast rifle-green; wing coverts glaucous-grey; tail ditto, with black bars, and fringed with dark chestnut. The cock is a perfect dandy, strutting with most dignified step. The hen is much more marked than the common pheasant, her whole plumage being of a richer brown, with dark, arrow-shaped markings on it, and a white spot under the eye.

Being true pheasants, Versicolors attain full plumage after the first moult. The eggs are smaller than the common pheasant's. The young require no special treatment; they are extremely fond of lettuce, and, before they are thirty-six hours old, will fairly bolt pieces certainly as large as a shilling—one is surprised how they get it down; at all times I think they are the largest feeders of any pheasant I have kept. During the breeding season, the males are most pugnacious, and will attack anyone when entering the pens; hence, they are not so easily tamed as other varieties. They are very apt to fly up on anyone going near the aviary; this causes them to strike their heads, and I have thus lost several valuable birds. You must, therefore, either cut one wing, or keep the birds in low aviaries, so that they do not attain sufficient impetus in flying to risk injury to their skulls. Keep three or four hens to a cock.

The Versicolors would not be so generally attractive as Reeves'; they are much smaller birds, and their colours are less conspicuous, but, perhaps, on the whole, the most beautiful. Some say they are very pugnacious, and drive away the other birds (a bad feature in coverts); but they cross very freely with the common pheasant, so much so, that in a short time the true breed would be lost, and we should have another cross, as we have between *Phasianus colchicus* and *P. torquatus* (or Chinese).

PEACOCK PHEASANTS
(*Polyplectron chinquis*).

CHAPTER XIV.

THE PEACOCK PHEASANT

(*Polyplectron chinquis*).

The Link between Peacocks and Pheasants — Shy Breeders—Colours—Difficulties of Breeding.

THESE birds appear to form the link between the peacocks and the pheasants. They are natives of Assam; their habits are shy, and, although they are very handsome, I do not think many will care to keep them. They are shy breeders, laying only two eggs for a brood. In their native state they breed four times a year. Their young, when hatched, follow closely behind the mother, keeping under her tail, which is spread fan-shaped.

The sexes are very similar. The head is grey, shaded into black; neck and breast brown, slightly pencilled with black; throat white; wings having the point of each feather with an eye of green of a lovely emerald colour, shaded with violet; back the colour of shoulders and neck. Each feather of the tail has the eye on it, similar to the wings. With the exception of this mark, the whole plumage is a quiet brown; legs green.

If we could manage to breed from acclimatised specimens, we should, probably, in a few generations, get quieter birds. I never succeeded in breeding these birds. I am informed the young get in the way of the feet of their foster-mother when a bantam is used, and she knocks them over when scratching, their habit being, as I before remarked, to keep close under the mother.

IMPEYAN PHEASANTS
(Lophophorus Impeyanus).

CHAPTER XV.

THE IMPEYAN PHEASANT
(*Lophophorus impeyanus*).

Where Common—Longevity—Peculiar Habits—Breeding in England—Colours of Cock—Colours of Hen—Feeding.

ON the high ground of the Himalayas these birds are very common. I do not know when the first living specimens were brought to England, but Mr. W. Jamrach has each year, for some time, past, imported some. They will live a long time, with ordinary care and attention to their habits, but they are not desirable birds in a limited space; they are great diggers, rooting up their aviaries in search of roots and buried corn. Many specimens have been bred in England, and I understand the Maharajah Dhuleep Singh was very desirous of introducing them on his estate. In India, they afford fine shooting, are much sought after, and, sad to say, large numbers are destroyed for their plumage.

The adult male has head dark green, with a plume

about 3in. long; each feather has its stem naked, and ending in a flat tuft; neck lovely red copper, very dark; shoulders brilliant metallic olive-green; saddle white, purple, and violet; tail cinnamon; wings black, with coverts of bright emerald-green; breast metallic green; belly black; legs dark ash. The hen is of a rich brown, in general marking somewhat the same as a woodcock, but lighter; throat white; legs ash-coloured. She lays mostly eight eggs, and will sit herself.

I kept my specimens for some time, but their untidy habits and my limited space compelled me to part with them. They are greedy feeders on chopped roots, such as carrots, turnips, &c., and must have plenty of green food. I believe they are always kept in pairs. Darwin states two hens will not agree.

CHAPTER XVI.

THE COMMON PHEASANT
(Phasianus colchicus).

Weight and Size—Colours of Cock—Colours of Hen—Change of Colour since Introduction—Colours of the Wild Bird—Pens: Site and Soil for; Construction of; Shelter in—Number of Hens to Cock—Another System for Pens—Pinioning and Cutting Wings—Doors for Pens—Building Pens in Blocks — Feeding — Hatching — Where Best to Place Coops — Young Birds Wandering — Change of Ground for Rearing — Coops: Shelter for; Moving—Watching the Birds—Feeding the Young—Water—Insect Food—The Chinese or Ring-neck—Prolificacy of the Common Pheasant—Desirable Varieties for the Game Preserver—The True P. colchicus—Elliot's " Monograph of Pheasants "—The Wallichii or Cheer Pheasant.

AS yet I have not written anything with reference to the common pheasant. The male weighs about 3lb., and is 3ft. in length. Bill pale yellowish horn-colour; irides yellow; sides of the head bare; the face crimson, minutely speckled with black, and the wattles, when excited, meeting on the top of the head; these wattles are considerably brighter during the breeding season, when the bird also erects tufts of feathers, resembling ears or horns, on either side of the head. The head is black-green, blue, and violet, ending in most cases, now, in a white collar or ring round the throat; this denotes contamination with the Chinese variety. The tail is cuneiform, and consists of eighteen feathers, the two middle sometimes 20in. long. The legs are blackish-brown, with the short, strong spur of all true pheasants. The saddle is now mostly greenish, varying according to the amount of cross-breeding; belly black; sides golden, with black spots. The female of the common bird is not as large as the male; she is of a rufous-brown, bill brown, irides hazel, and the sides of head feathered; tail same shape as the male, but not so long.

Such is a somewhat rough description of the common pheasant of the present day. They are totally different to what they were when first introduced to this country, and hardly any two are alike. A year or two ago I was fortunate enough to obtain a skin from Trans-Caucasia; this was exhibited at a meeting of the Zoological Society, and was regarded by Mr. Seebohm, Mr. Dresser, and other authorities, as a genuine example of the pure *P. colchicus*, as it existed in this country before it was so greatly changed by crossing with other species, so as no longer to exist in a pure state. The wild bird is much darker, the whole colouring inclined to dark, rich red, the sides being very dark, with small, black spots, instead of the large ones now seen on the common pheasants; the tail also being particularly well marked with dark, rich bars, and fringed with maroon-red; saddle red, no sign of grey, as in the modern pheasant.

In this chapter I propose to place before my readers a few of the plans adopted for breeding this variety, leaving it to them to select the one they fancy to be best suited to their requirements.

Most—I think I may say all—breeders object to permanent pens; they like each year to put the birds on fresh ground. The site requires great care in selection; it should be on moderately sloping land, certainly well drained, and as free as possible from anything likely to disturb the birds. Perhaps old turf is as good as anything: it is generally recommended to break up this turf, so that impurities will the more readily be absorbed. The best subsoil is gravel; the worst, stiff clay. The pens are all the better for the shelter of a belt of firs; and it is very desirable, if possible, that they be placed near the keeper's cottage, so that he may at all times be able to keep an eye on them.

Place stout posts in the ground, standing 4ft. or 5ft. out; to these either nail wire netting, or slabs, or boards. One of the plans recommended is to board or slab up from the bottom, say 2ft. 6in., and finish above this with 2in. wire netting. Great care must be taken to let the boards into the ground so as to prevent vermin working in; or you can have hurdles made of strips of beech or oak; these can easily be fixed to the posts, and removed at the end of the season; the strips stand upright, and must be, say, 2in. wide, 1in. thick, and 1in. apart. Many breeders continue the wire quite into the ground, protecting the outside with gorse and brambles; but this is hardly as safe from foxes, dogs, &c., as boards. The size of the pens is, in many cases, only 12ft. by 12ft.; this is scarcely large enough—they certainly ought not to be less than 14ft. square, and if larger, so much the better. It was purposely said that the posts are to be 4ft. or 5ft. out of the ground, because it is a debated point whether there is any advantage, when they are going to be wired at the tops, in having them too high. The birds are more likely to get impetus in flying in a high place, and to kill themselves by striking the head. They will require but little shelter. Place a pole or two across the pen, supported on two forks, and against this lean faggots sloping both ways; it is a great advantage if you can make some slope to the sun, for the birds to dust and bask under. It is presumed this pen will be wired over, with a support or two in it to carry the netting. You can do this in small pens by nailing cross-pieces on a pole like the points of a weathercock. In this pen, if closed at top, put a cock and five or six hens; perhaps the former is the better number.

Another system is to inclose a far larger space, according to situation, &c., leaving it open on the top, and placing a number of hens in it with cut wings. Some persons pinion the hens, but the disadvantage is that these birds cannot be afterwards turned out. The birds will require their wings cut every three weeks, or they will escape. If a proper place has been chosen, the hens will be visited by the wild cocks.

All the pens will require a door placed in one side. Of course, if the first plan is adopted, and a large number of pens are required, it will greatly reduce the cost to build them in a block; they thus form the sides of each other, and in some cases three of the sides, or even four, if a large number are built.

The birds should be well fed, but not so much so as to render them fat. Maize, wheat, and abundance of green food, should form the staple diet. Pheasants enjoy a swede or turnip, savoy, chickweed—in fact, almost any fresh, green food. They must be well supplied with water, to which you will, of course, add a little tonic, like the sulphate of iron mixture, at times. When they commence to lay, a sharp look-out must be kept for the eggs. Most eggs are laid in the latter part of the day or early in the morning. When the birds are in full lay is the time to keep up their strength, and, for this purpose, nothing is better than Spratts Crissel, added to boiled potatoes, barley-meal, waste scraps of the house, &c. Boiled rice is also good. Think how very monotonous the food of penned birds is, when we compare it with the little delicacies supplied by Nature.

Some writers advocate the placing of coops round the keeper's house, propping up the sliding door, and otherwise encouraging the hens intended to rear the pheasants to lay in them, and, as soon as one of them is wishing to sit, substituting pheasant eggs for her own. I cannot suggest any more natural plan. She will then come off and return as Nature prompts her, and will require only to be shut in and protected just as the eggs are due to hatch. No turning, no sprinkling, nothing required: Nature will do all.

Hatching has been fully treated in Chapter III. When the birds are fit to remove to the field, the coops —which should have been ready placed for the hens on properly-selected ground—will at once receive them. Nothing is better than good old grass—well-drained, of course. No cattle must be allowed in the meadow, and care must be taken that they cannot get in, or vast mischief will soon arise. Lucerne is even preferable to grass; but both must be kept well cut, so as to leave open spaces for the coops; and the same applies to clover.

I must repeat my caution with regard to looking after the young birds when they are let out of the coop for the first time; they are so silly, they rush out with head erect, wander off, and are lost because they do not know the hen's call—and some hens have but very little voice. At first it is certainly best to inclose the coop with a few yards of fine netting, so that the chicks cannot get into the long grass and be lost. This will only be required for the first few days; when once they know the hen's call, they will come back to her.

All that has been written on the treatment of the foreign varieties equally applies to the common pheasant. It is very desirable that young birds should not be reared each year, or certainly more than two years at the most, on the same ground. It is not so much a matter of taint in the soil, as that insects will, in a great measure, have been destroyed, and young birds cannot thrive without these. No doubt some localities are far more suitable to the production of insects than others, and it is these that best suit young birds. Hot gravels and baking clay are alike most unsuitable; neither are bare and exposed places fit; but well-sheltered hillsides, sloping to south-west, are to be preferred.

The coops are generally placed in lines, or in such form as will best enable the keeper to attend to them. It is very desirable that there be some bushes, either natural or artificial, to which the young birds can retreat in case of alarm from crows or hawks. The coops should be shaded with green boughs in very hot weather, and moved every day, or even twice a day, on to fresh ground. All the instructions given in previous chapters as to damp under coops, protection, &c., will have to be observed; also those with regard to food and water.

Should there be any need to change the situation of the coops, the instructions previously given as to shutting in the birds will readily enable you to do this, and the form of coop and run illustrated (Fig. 3) will be found very suitable.

In large establishments, the birds are never left night or day, a keeper sleeping in a hut on the ground, so as to be prepared for poachers, or any vermin. Some shepherd-dogs are very destructive, and as they are constantly about the farm, can work great mischief in a very quiet way. If anything goes wrong, these dogs should be carefully watched.

Food is the same as mentioned in previous chapters. Perhaps it will be well not to tempt the young from under their mother before the dew is off the grass in the morning. Get the birds off luxuries as soon as you can, inducing them to eat wheat, hemp, canary, or any whole corn. Let them have plenty of onions; there is no food better for, or more liked by, young birds; they are even preferred to lettuce.

Many keepers throw food broadcast; but although it is well to do so with a little, so as to teach the young to forage, perhaps it is best to put the principal part on little trays or saucers of tin or wood, kept very clean; the saving in food will pay for cleaning.

As the birds grow, they get more independent, and the coops will have to be moved towards the coverts, into which the young will gradually work. The birds are still to be fed round the coops, and by degrees will stray away, and no longer come in to roost; when this is the case the hen can be removed.

The vexed question of water being given or withheld is left to the reader. I strongly advocate plenty of clean, spring water, taken away, at first, after each feeding, lest the birds stand in it and get cramp.

There is no doubt that, when birds are failing, consequent on a dry, cold season, or a very hot one, nothing helps them so much as plenty of ants' eggs or well-scoured maggots; but beware of these latter, unless well scoured, as they are sure to produce diarrhœa.

The Chinese, or Ring-necks, are undoubtedly the most prolific layers; but they are also the most inveterate wanderers. It is said the old dark birds are not so easy to rear as these; on this I am not able to form a positive opinion. The old dark, or bronze, bird is by most people admired; but the Chinese is rapidly removing, by its intermixture, all traces of the original bird we had from the Thasis river many centuries ago. You very seldom see a bird at a game-dealer's that has not a large taint of Chinese blood, and during the last ten years I have examined thousands.

Towards the end of July, 1885, some eggs of the common pheasant were given me, which had been found while mowing some late clover. These were hatched 12th August; I reserved five hens, placing them with an adult hen and a young cock. They began to lay 14th April, and up to 25th June, 1886, had laid 248 eggs; they continued to lay until the second week in August, by which time they had produced over seventy eggs each. The eggs up to June 25th went to a friend; the remainder I set, and hatched at the rate of twelve, and even fourteen, birds out of every fifteen eggs. So these prolific birds proved that, when well fed and cared for, even though late hatched, they make good stock pheasants. Probably they would have died in a wild state, being too weakly to withstand the wet and cold of autumn.

I am hoping to re-introduce the original breed of pheasant—the true *Colchicus*. He is a dark bird, of course without the ring on neck; that came from China, and it is found as you approach Europe the ring gradually ceases, and when we get to Asia Minor we have a fine, handsome bird, larger than the Ring-neck of China.

CHAPTER XVII.

THE CHINESE PHEASANT
(Phasianus torquatus).

The Common Pheasant of China—Origin of Specific Name—Abundant Layers—Wandering Habits—Colours of a Pure Specimen—Colours of Hen.

THIS bird appears to be the common pheasant of China, and is met with all over that country; thousands are said to be exposed for sale in the markets. It obtains its specific name from the white ring on the neck. I believe it was one of the first varieties brought to England after *P. colchicus,* and it has now spread all over the country; in very few, if any, districts are birds found free from the ring on the neck. They are smaller than the old sort, and persons who have eaten the pure bred say they are not equal to them in flavour. They are much preferred by those who trade in eggs, as being more abundant layers, and easier to rear; but game-preservers give them a bad character, as they wander so much. This is a most undesirable habit. One does not like to breed and protect pheasants which take every opportunity of going off one's land; and some neighbours are not so scrupulous as they might be, and encourage them to do so, aided by raisins, potatoes, &c. I prefer, for cold districts, a dash of the Chinese blood, as they are undoubtedly very hardy.

It is said that the Chinese birds now in St. Helena have considerably changed in colour from the true stock left there very many years ago. The following are the colours of a pure specimen, now before me, which came direct from China. Forehead bronze-green; back of head and face dark green with blue shade; ears long, and very dark green; collar pure white, $\frac{1}{3}$in. deep, rather widest at the points of shoulders; behind collar the green continues for a margin, then shades off on back to light brown, deeply edged with green; back creamy-white, each feather having a wide margin of reddish-brown; saddle grey-green, with its sides a fine glaucous-grey, fringed with light chestnut; shoulders and wing coverts exactly the colour of side of saddle; breast deep reddish-brown, edged with black, and getting paler, and markings larger, towards belly, which, in the centre, is deep green; sides of body very light brown, with large, black markings; feet and legs jet black; wings dark brown, each feather edged with red; tail olive-brown, fringed with reddish-violet and barred with black—the bars get wider as they approach the tail point, and terminate in fully 2in. of black point. The whole bird has a green-grey appearance, when compared with the common pheasant. The hen is decidedly lighter in general appearance than the hen of the common pheasant, but otherwise is very like her. I have imported hens from their native home in the Caucasus, and also from China, and they are very similar to the common pheasant of this country; but the hen of the Versicolor is much darker and smaller, and could not be mistaken for either of the others.

CHAPTER XVIII.

CROSSES, AND IMPORTING SPECIMENS.

Crossing—Amherst Cock and Gold Hen: Value of; Plumage of—Other Crosses: Gold and Common; Silver and Common Fowl; Common and Domestic Fowl; Reeves' and Common—Table of Results of Various Crosses—Importation of Foreign Pheasants: Mr. Jamrach's Letter on Results of.

BY mating an Amherst cock with a Gold hen you will obtain a bird of which the male may well be said to far surpass either parent in beauty. A few years ago, a male of this cross sold at Antwerp for £37. The following will briefly describe a male in full plumage: Crest orange; iris white; face pale straw-colour; tippet black and white, like the Amherst; breast red, with buff feathers at the point of shoulder; tail feathers having enlarged black spots, rest of feathers like the Gold; saddle yellow, with red-orange at base of tail. The hen is very similar to a pure Amherst, but has less chestnut on the head.

Subjoined are a few remarks on other crosses of pheasants. Of the cross between the Gold and the common pheasant I have heard of many instances, and I can depend on them. I have met with a hybrid between the Silver and the common fowl. A cross known to almost every keeper, from the cocks visiting his poultry, is that of the common pheasant with the domestic fowl. Amherst and Gold produce a grand bird, which readily breeds again, either *inter se* or with either parent breed, and so produces endless varieties, some favouring the Gold, others the Amherst. Reeves' and the common sort interbreed freely, but I do not know of any instance in which the cross has bred again. I have found, with both Elliot and Sœmmerring, that, when crossed with the common pheasant, not a single egg hatched.

The following list exhibits the results of various crosses:

Crosses.	Eggs.
Gold and common pheasant	Fertile.
Silver and domestic fowl	Fertile.
Common pheasant and domestic fowl	Fertile.
Amherst and Gold	Fertile.
Reeves' and common	Fertile.
Elliot and common	Unfertile.
Sœmmerring and common	Unfertile.
Versicolor and Gold	Unfertile.

The following extract from a letter of Mr. W. Jamrach may give some idea of the difficulty experienced in bringing to this country the several varieties we now possess. I think that all bird-lovers are under great obligations to Mr. Jamrach. The manner in which, year after year, he has persevered, and that, too, under heavy losses, in his endeavours to import rare pheasants, should win the gratitude of all fanciers. His efforts were at last crowned with success, but not, I fear, with the pecuniary reward he so richly deserves. He says: "In 1864 I left India with 20 Impeyans and Tragopans; 7 only survived. 1867 and '68, 300, by the old overland route; all died. Ditto, 285, with same results. 1869, 100, by Suez Canal; 40 survived. From that time to the present I have annually brought over successfully a number of pheasants, including Argus, Tragopans, various *Euplocami*, Pucras, Impeyans, &c. In 1879 I first introduced *Gallophasis Ellioti*, and sold the pair for 3000f., and for five years pursued with ardour their introduction, at a cost of 10,000f. The difficulties were almost insurmountable, but were at last overcome, and there are now a few pairs in England. The importation of these rare birds is not so profitable as it appears, for I have lost, during the nineteen years I have been engaged in these transactions, no less than £3000, or 75,000f."

CHAPTER XIX.

DISEASES, ETC.

Gapes: Inhalation of Carbolic Acid Fumes for—Scaly Legs—Roup—Ophthalmia—Cramp—Scrofulous Disease—Boarded Floors and Leg Weakness—Fractures—Lice—Ovarian Disease and Soft Eggs.

THE diseases of pheasants are much the same as those of poultry, and require similar treatment. No doubt some seasons induce certain forms of disease more than others, as, for instance, ophthalmia, roup, cramp, &c.

Gapes.—This is the great pest of pheasant-breeders; but, strange as it may appear, I have never had a case. How this happens I know not; but so it is. There are various remedies now before the public, and some are well spoken of, and believed to be cures. Probably, inhalation of carbolic acid fumes is one of the best; but great care must be exercised in not keeping the bird too long in the box. The following is the method pursued: Construct a box having a perforated false bottom about half-way up its sides. Then make a brick quite hot, place the box over it, and drop about five or six drops of carbolic acid on the brick. When the fumes arise, place the bird in the box, close the lid for a few seconds, and, on removal to the fresh air, the patient should be none the worse, and the worm destroyed.

Scaly Legs.—The best plan is to rub off the rough scurf, even if it makes the leg bleed. Glycerine applied to the place where the scurf has been is a good remedy; sulphur ointment is also a useful application. The disease often arises from the silky hens under which the pheasants are reared. Versicolors are afflicted with this disease more frequently than any other variety I have kept; but attention and cleanliness will soon cure it.

Roup.—Follow the same treatment as for fowls. Keep the birds in a warm, dry place. If you have young birds affected with this ailment in wet seasons, feed them on toast steeped in ale, keep their eyes and nostrils well sponged with very weak vinegar and water, and you will hardly lose a bird. They must be very liberally fed with most nourishing food. Roup is undoubtedly the result of severe cold, and nothing but warmth and stimulating food will enable a pheasant to survive it; otherwise the bird dies of weakness and exhaustion. The first sign is slight swelling of the head; then a froth appears at the corner of the eye: this arises from the passage to the nostrils being choked. Next, this froth becomes thicker, takes the form of matter, and is offensive.

And so the disease develops, from what was at first only a cold, till it becomes severe roup, and most infectious ; but long ere this the bird should be removed from its fellows.

Ophthalmia.—The year 1886 had, undoubtedly, a sad notoriety for this disease, which leads one to think it is induced by certain climatic influences. The best remedy is to paint the eyes two or three times daily with a weak solution of nitrate of silver (about three grains to an ounce of water). I have also heard of the roof of the mouth being painted with it, but can offer no opinion on this.

Cramp is, in many cases, induced by cold and wet, but, no doubt, also arises from a disordered stomach. The remedy is to keep the birds warm and dry, and, if the coops are in a damp situation, to be sure and use the boards mentioned under the head of "Coops," in Chapter II.; these are far preferable to sacking, which is very apt to get soaked, and is then difficult to dry. Half-grown birds are as often taken with cramp as young birds; they seem to lose the use of their legs, and become quite helpless.

Scrofulous Disease is often brought about by inbreeding, and from mating unhealthy birds. There can be only one remedy for this—pure, fresh blood, and strong and healthy stock. Weed out all weak birds, selecting only the best to breed from. Take every precaution to promote health and vigour.

One season I was much troubled with the birds' mouths being full of froth. I could not trace it in any way, but suspected that it arose from some blight. Keepers say it comes from " Cuckoo-spit," the blight so frequently found on lavender bushes.

It is said that boarded floors, if young birds are kept too long on them, produce leg-weakness. I do not object to a little short straw or broken hay on the board, only it must not be allowed to get damp. Remember, when the birds are getting their tail feathers, and their wings are large and heavy, they will require ample and nutritious feeding. Much depends on season and weather: cold, dry weather, and no insects, are conditions very trying to young birds; mild, damp, showery, but not too wet weather, suits them best. I quite agree with Mr. Tegetmeier on the folly of too close interbreeding, for it rapidly degenerates the birds.

Fractures very readily take place in young pheasants, and are caused by the birds flying about in the aviaries. I have cured many broken legs, and some fractured thighs. An Impeyan broke his thigh soon after I bought him; it was set in plaster splints, when he entirely recovered, and became a fine bird. The limbs must be carefully set, and bound up with narrow strips of linen. The assistance of a medical friend will be of much service if you have no knowledge of bone-setting yourself, as you will probably find the limb heal, and the bird be a cripple for life, if the leg is not correctly set. The patient should be placed by himself, disturbed as little as possible, well fed, and kept clean. If the fracture is properly set, the invalid will probably recover.

Lice.—Vermin troubling the young birds, in the shape of lice, can easily be exterminated by using insect-powder. The lice are usually found under the wings and thighs, and on the head, and are no doubt given by the old hens. Dressing the breasts with sweet oil is a great preventive; also, whilst setting, you can sprinkle the nest with insect-powder. I do not like hay for nests; it becomes full of vermin. Notice the nest of a wild hen, and try to make yours like it.

Soft eggs are the result of ovarian disease, frequently promoted by over-feeding. Do not forget that lime, such as old mortar, should be placed in the pens, or some slacked lime put in the drinking-water.

CHAPTER XX.

CATCHING BIRDS, PACKING, ETC.

Catching Birds—Use of the Net—Method of Handling Birds—Packing Birds—The Best Basket—How to Furnish Baskets—Division of the Basket—Packing Eggs.

CATCHING BIRDS.

A SMALL net, strained on a hoop the shape of a racquet, but with a rather longer handle, so that the birds cannot turn when in it, is the best to use. This is easily made of a forked hazel or ash stick. Press the birds firmly to the ground. Never seize by the legs until you have your other hand well over the back and wings. Never swing birds by the legs, as cruel people do chickens; take them by the thighs, and not by the legs.

PACKING BIRDS.

The best baskets are round, about 1ft. deep, and vary in diameter according to number and size of birds. It is not well to pack too many birds in a basket; they tread on each others' tails, and in every way spoil their appearance. The baskets should be canvas-covered, and a handle, formed of one stout osier, is very serviceable. If the weather is cold, they are best canvas-lined inside. Put a little chopped straw, say 4in. in length, at the bottom; this is better than hay, which is very apt to twist round the birds' legs. But best of all are the needles, or spines, of fir-trees. If the birds are going very long journeys, stitch a piece or two of cabbage to the inside of the basket; being moist, this serves the purpose of both food and water. If many birds are placed in one basket, it is best to have a division across the middle; this can be formed of canvas.

PACKING EGGS.

It is generally admitted that, for this purpose, nothing is better than clean, dry moss, twisted neatly round each egg. The eggs should be placed in wooden boxes, and not allowed to shake about.

CHAPTER XXI.

A WALK ROUND MY AVIARIES.

Calls of the Different Varieties—Gaudy Plumage and Harsh Voices—The Amherst and his Tail—Elliots: Pugnacity of; Handsome Appearance of; Love-making of—Versicolors: Pride of; Varied Dispositions of—Golds: Hardiness of; Restless Motion of—A Pugnacious Reeves' Cock—Capturing a Lost Bird—The True Phasianus Colchicus—Desirable Varieties for the Game Preserver—How to Prevent Sœmmerring Cocks Destroying their Hens—Pheasant Literature: Elliot's "Monograph of Pheasants."

ON both sides of my house I have my aviaries, seventeen in number, and, as I sit reading or writing, I know the calls of the birds as they utter their various notes of love or warfare. Sometimes it is the harsh note of a Versicolor cock as he crows, ending in an "oh!" after first flapping his wings, a feat which all pheasants perform. No sooner has he crowed, than the challenge is taken up either by a common pheasant, whose crow is familiar to every sportsman, or by the quiet "chuckle,

chuckle," of the Reeves' and his wives, who generally have a word to say whenever their lord speaks. Then my true pheasants (*Phasianus colchicus*) from the Caucasus crow; their note is not so loud or so defiant as that of their English brothers, but probably when older it will be deeper. The screeching note of the Amherst is mostly heard towards evening, and that of the Gold at all hours; both these have most discordant voices: as with most birds, the gaudier their plumage the harsher their voice.

Now come with me and look at some of these aviaries. In No. 1 (which was for many years occupied by Old Amherst, from whom I bred a very large number of birds each year, and whose skin has now gone to the Natural History Museum, South Kensington), there is now a fine young Amherst, a descendant of the old bird, and it is a pleasure to see how elegantly he manages his splendid long tail, so coveted by salmon fishers. As I enter the aviary, and give him and his quietly-dressed wife some hemp seed or lettuce, they are not in the least afraid of me, provided I wear my old keeper's coat, for, if dressed differently, they at once know it.

In the next three aviaries are Elliots. They are not so tame, and spend most of their time in endeavouring to fight each other through the boarded partitions; they flap their wings in a different way to most birds, doing it continuously and very rapidly, as the Swinhoes do; but this only occurs early in the breeding season, when they also spread their tails fan fashion. They are most lovely birds, with their well-shaped, snake-like heads of silver, grey, and black, rich copper backs, and white bars or braces crossed. It is a most absurd sight to see an Elliot cock making love; he dances and jumps round and round the hen, then takes a scamper, and again jumps and bounds high in the air round her, his wattles erected to a perfect point, as in the case of the Swinhoe. In many of his actions he is very like that bird.

Now we come to a pen of one cock and three hen Versicolors. Here Beauty, the cock, no sooner sees me than he erects his ears like horns, and, making his rich red wattles, studded with minute feathers, to meet, and extending them deeply also below his throat, he walks up and down before me, displaying all his bright colours, elevating first one side of his body and then the other, so as to display all his beauty, as he would to a hen when courting her; but the instant I attempt to enter, he puts himself in a fighting attitude, dashes at me, and would rip my trousers, or, if I stooped, strike me in the face, so high does he spring; and when I retreat, he crows again and again in token of victory, and flies repeatedly against the wire netting to try to get at me. The next aviary has a similar number, but the cock is altogether as quiet and well-behaved as the last was pugnacious. In the next is Dandy, my old bird, and the father of Beauty; he is so proud that he walks on tiptoe, erecting himself till his head is quite perpendicular, and his tail drags the ground. He is a glorious bird, truly versicolor, for his coat is of all shades and colours, and shines like metal in the sun. His quietly-dressed wives, in their becoming plumage of shades of black and brown, have a fine green sheen on their backs and shoulders. What colours can surpass these? Notice the grouse, the partridge, the quail, and all the birds having shades of black and brown; how well these assimilate with the ground, and what protection they afford to the sitting hen!

Now we go to the other side of the house. In the first aviary are eighteen Gold cocks in full plumage, living entirely in the open, exposed to the North wind, roosting with their heads under their wings, and very often with the snow on their backs. Nothing hurts them; they are as hardy as Cossacks, and show incessant, restless motion all day, as they dance round each other, and display their rich colour (it is a bachelor establishment) to each other, delighting their many visitors—for, being in the carriage-drive, they see many people. Nothing disturbs them, from a coal-waggon to a carriage; every errand boy stops to look at them. No matter, they dance and flirt quite regardless who looks on. They feed from the hand, and seem perfectly happy. The next aviary has not quite so many, and, being less conspicuous, the birds are shyer.

We now come to a pen of Reeves'. Here I dare not enter without a switch, for Beaconsfield, as we call him, because his motto is *semper paratus*, at once prepares to drive me out. We have had many fights:

once I stunned him by accident, and once he slipped out after me to attack me, darted at me, and then flew away. Here was a fix—it was a foggy May morning, about 5 a.m. However, I felt sure he would not go far from his wives, so I made his loss known, and offered a reward. I soon had reports from all directions round that he had been seen, and by 6 p.m. the following day I recovered him quite uninjured— captured in a gravel pit—and restored him to his family. He is a truly superb bird, clean-built, with black, shining legs, very firm and hard, and a spur that would rip up anything. He is very tame so long as you are outside his domain—but you must not enter— and he is very troublesome when you collect the eggs. He has four beautiful hens, of great size; truly they are, as Lord Tweedmouth says, " Majesticus," and that should be their name. One of my cocks is just 6ft. long!

Some of the true *Phasianus colchicus* are to be seen in the next aviary. These are some of the birds imported from the Phasis river, the original home of our English pheasant; they are hardly so large as our birds, but look like great flyers. They are of the darkest, richest colour possible, with fine coppery backs and necks, red maroon saddle, and the same on the fringe of the tail. I have great hopes of being able to re-establish our original bird—a rich red, dark-breasted bird, free from Chinese taint. I have a pen or two of our common pheasants, one pen of which averaged seventy eggs each last year, and the birds were not one year old, having been hatched only the previous August; and again this year I have birds as large as any two-year-olds, although they were not hatched till the middle of August, 1886, and which are laying, and have laid since 10th April. In a wild state they would have died; but being well fed, and every care taken during the first part of the autumn, they soon got strong enough to do as well as the early-hatched birds.

I have several other aviaries, but I have now given up Impeyans, Firebacks, Swinhoes, Peacocks, &c., and go in more for varieties of the true *Phasianidæ*, because they come into full plumage the first year.

I wish I could induce game-preservers to go more into some of our new varieties; there is no reason why the Reeves', Versicolor, and, in a year or two, the Elliot, might not be more generally bred than they are. The two former have been tried on some estates; but, on the whole, these fine breeds have not met with the encouragement they deserve. Sœmmerrings, although true pheasants, have never made much progress, owing, it is thought, to the cocks so frequently killing the hens. This would not be the case in preserves; it is the close quarters, and lack of means to escape by hiding, that tempt the cock to destroy the hen in captivity.

In bringing this book to a close, I can only add— the more I see of these birds the more I admire them, and believe they will amply repay anyone who will devote as much time and attention to them as I have.

Those taking an interest in pheasants should study that magnificent folio, Elliot's "Monograph of Pheasants." In it they will find full descriptions of *Mongolicus, Insignis,* two varieties of Sœmmerrings, the Impeyans, Pucras, Tragopans, and other species.

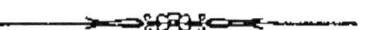

INDEX.

A.

Adaptability of pheasants for breeding and rearing in towns, 1
Amherst and his tail, the, 85
Amhersts, Lady, 39
    Screeching notes of, 85
Aviaries, a walk round my, 84
    Cleaning, 8
    Doors for, 8
    Permanent, 4
    Permanent, dimensions of, 4
    Permanent drainage of, 7
    Permanent-erecting, 4-8
    Permanent, perches for, 8
    Permanent, planting shrubs in front of, 7
    Permanent, shape of, 4
    Permanent, soil for, 4
    Portable, 9, 11
    Portable, cost of, 12
    Portable, dimensions of, 11
    Portable, for young birds, 12
    Portable, how to make, 11
    Water for, 11

B.

Baskets for packing birds, 82
    For packing, furnishing and fitting, 83
Beauty of Golds, 2
Birds, catching, 82
    Eating eggs, plans to cure, 18
    Method of handling, 82

Birds, packing, 82
    When to obtain, 3
Bottom boards for coops, advantages of, 14
Breeding, 17
    And rearing in towns, adaptability of pheasants for, 1
    And rearing Reeves', 47, 48
    Golds, 36
    Lady Amhersts, 40
    Pens for common pheasants, erecting, 63
    Pens for common pheasants, shelter for, 63, 64
    Pens for common pheasants, site and soil for, 63
    The common pheasant, 63
    Time for, 3

C.

Calls of the different varieties, 84
Capital required for keeping and breeding pheasants, small, 3
Catching birds, 82
    Birds, net for, 82
Chickens, feeding, 29
    Straying, how to prevent, 30
    Treatment of, immediately after hatching, 26
    When and how to feed, 30
Chinese, 71
    Abundant laying powers of, 71
    Colours of a pure specimen, 72
    Origin of specific name of, 71

Chinese, or Ring-necks, inveterate wandering of, 69, 71
Chipped eggs, how to treat, 25
Cleaning aviaries, 8
Colchicus, the true, 70
Collecting eggs, 19
Common pheasants, 61
    Breeding, 63
    Breeding, in inclosed runs left open at top, 64
    Breeding, in pens, 63
    Care needed to prevent chicks straying, 66
    Change in colours of, since introduction, 62
    Colours of cocks, 61
    Colours of hens, 62
    Feeding, 65
    How to place coops for, 67
    Insect food for, 69
    Modes of feeding young birds, 68
    Moving coops to fresh ground, 67
    Number of hens to cock, 64
    Prolificacy of, 69
    Shelter for coops, 67
    Treatment of sitting hens, 66
    Treatment of young birds, 66
    Watching young birds, 68
    Water for, 68
    Weight and size of, 61
Concrete floors, 7
Coop and run, 13
Coops, 13
    Advantages of bottom boards for, 14
    Cost of, 14
    Dimensions of, 13
    How best to change soiled boards in, 15
    How to make, 13
    How to render vermin-proof, 14
    Use of netting for, 14
Cost of portable aviary, 12
Country-house, pheasants an attraction to the grounds of, 1
Cramp, 79
Creepers, planting, in front of permanent aviaries, 7
Crosses, 74

Crosses, Amherst cock and gold hen, colours of, 74
    Common pheasant and domestic fowl, 75
    Elliot and common pheasant, 75
    Gold and common, 74
    Reeves' and common pheasant, 75
    Results of various, 75
    Silver and common fowl, 75
    Sœmmerring and common pheasant, 75
Cutting the wings of young birds, 31

D.

Damping eggs, 24
Diarrhœa in young birds, 31
Dimensions of coops, 13
    Of permanent aviary, 4
    Of portable aviary, 11
    Of runs, 14
Diseases, 77
    Cramp, 79
    Gapes, 77
    Fractures, 80
    Leg weakness, 80
    Lice, 81
    Ophthalmia, 79
    Roup, 78
    Scaly legs, 78
    Scrofula, 79
    Soft eggs, 81
Doors for aviaries, 8
Drainage of permanent aviary, 7
Drinking-water, tonic for, 17
Dust-bath, 8

E.

Egg-eating, plans to cure, 18
    The habit of, how acquired, 18
    Varieties most addicted to, 18
Egg-protector, advantages of using, 25
    Christy's, 25
    Use of, 25
Eggs, collecting, 19
    Damping, 24

Index.

Eggs, number of, to set, 20
    Packing, 83
    Setting, 19
    Testing, 25
Elliot's "Monograph of Pheasants," 90
Elliots, 52
    Colours of cocks, 52
    Colours of hens, 52
    General appearance of, 52
    Good points of, 53
    Hardiness of, 53
    Introduction of, 52
    Love-making of, 86
    Number of eggs laid by hen, 53
    Number of hens to cock, 53
    Pugnacity of, 85
    Rarity of, 53
Erecting a permanent aviary, 4-8
Euplocamus nycthemerus, 37
    Prelatus, 50
    Swinhœi, 42

F.

Feeding, 19
    Chickens, 29
    Common pheasants, 65
    Laying hens, 19
Fertility, testing eggs for, 25
Fishermen, value of plumage of Golds to, 34
    Value of plumage of Lady Amhersts to, 40
Floors, concrete, 9
Food for laying hens, 17
    Recommended for chickens, 30
Foreign pheasants an attraction to the grounds of a country-house, 1
Fractures, 80

G.

Gallophasis Ellioti, 52
Game-preserver, varieties desirable for the, 89
Gapes, 77
    Treatment of, by inhalation of carbolic acid fumes, 77

Gaudy plumage and harsh voices, 85
Golds, 34
    Beauty of, 2
    Breeding, 36
    Buying young cocks of, 2
    Causes of popularity of, 34
    Colours of cocks, 35
    Colours of hens, 35
    Grace in movement of, 36
    Hardiness of, 2, 11
    Hardiness of my, 87
    Incessant restless motion of, 87
    Introduction of, 34
    Kept in the open, 2
    Moderate cost of, 2
    Number of hens to cock, 36
    Pugnacity of cocks, 35
    Restless disposition of, 34
    Roosting in the open, 2
    Special advantages of keeping, 35
    Splendid plumage of, 36
    Suitability of, as pets, 35
    Value of plumage of, 34

H.

Handling birds, method of, 82
Hardiness of Golds, 2, 11
    Of Lady Amhersts, 40
Harsh voices and gaudy plumage, 85
Hatching, 25
    How to assist, 25
Hens for sitting, best, 19
    Laying, 17
    Off their eggs, 23
    Sitting, treatment of, 20
How aviaries should face, 8

I.

Impeyans, 59
    Colours of cocks, 59
    Colours of hens, 60
    Feeding, 60
    Longevity of, 59
    Number of eggs laid by hen, 60
    Number of hens to cock, 60

Impeyans, peculiar habits of, 59
Importing specimens, 75
    Specimens, Mr. Jamrach's letter on the difficulties of, 75
Incubator, placing eggs near hatching in, 27
Inhalation of carbolic acid fumes for gapes, 77

J.

Jamrach's, Mr., letter on the difficulty of importing specimens, 75
Japanese, the, 54

L.

Lady Amhersts, 39
    Breeding, 40
    Cocks, tyrannical nature of, 16
    Colours of cocks, 40
    Colours of hens, 40
    Food for, 41
    Hardiness of, 40
    Introduction of, 39
    Number of hens to cock, 41
    Price of, 3
    Quarrelsome nature of, 41
    Suitability of, for rearing in a wild state, 39
Layers, the earliest, 17
Laying hens, 17
    Hens, best foods for, 19
    Hens, feeding, 19
    Hens, food for, 17
    Hens, shelter for, 17
    Hens, treatment of, 17
    In the open, dangers of, 18
    Period for, 17
Leg weakness and boarded floors, 80
Lice, 81
Literature, pheasant, 90
Lophophorus Impeyanus, 59
Love-making of Elliots, 86

M.

"Monograph of Pheasants," Eliot's, 90

N.

Nest, making the, 22
Number of eggs to set, 20

O.

Old Amherst, 85
Open aviary, keeping Golds in an, 2
Ophthalmia, 79

P.

Packing baskets, furnishing and fitting, 83
    Birds, 82
    Birds, baskets for, 82
    Birds closely to be avoided, 82
    Eggs, 83
Peacocks, 57
    Colours of, 57
    Difficulties of breeding, 58
    Habits of, in native country, 57
    Shy breeders, 57
    Similarity in colours of sexes, 57
Pen, portable, for young birds, 12
Pens in blocks, 65
Perches for permanent aviaries, 8
Permanent aviaries, 4
    Aviaries, perches for, 8
    Aviaries, planting creepers in front of, 7
    Aviaries, planting shrubs in front of, 7
    Aviaries, soil for, 4
    Aviary, dimensions of, 4
    Aviary, drainage of, 7
    Aviary, erecting a, 4, 8
    Aviary, shape of, 4
Persecution of hens by cock, how to avoid, 16
Phasianus colchicus, 61
    Colchicus, the true, 88
    Reevesii, 46
    Sœmmerringii, 44
    Torquatus, 71
    Versicolor, 54
Polyplectron chinquis, 57
Portable aviaries, 11

Index. 95

Portable aviaries for young birds, 12
   Aviaries, how to make, 11
   Aviary, 9
   Aviary, cost of, 12
   Aviary, dimensions of, 11
Putting out the young birds and hen, 28

R.

Rearing, 28
Reeves', 46
   Breeding and rearing, 47, 48
   Chuckling call of, 85
   Cock, a pugnacious, 87
   Colours of cocks, 47
   Colours of hens, 47
   Eating their eggs, how to prevent, 48
   Eggs of, 47
   Feeding, 48
   Introduction of, 46
   Number of eggs laid by hen, 48
   Number of hens to cock, 48
   Packing, 49
   Pugnacity of cocks, 48
   Singular calling noise and chuckling of, 48
   Tail of, 47
   "The pheasant of the future," 49
"Rocketers," 48
Roup, 78
Run, coop and, 13
Runs, dimensions of, 14
   How to make, 14

S.

Scaly legs, 78
Scope of work, 3
Scrofulous disease, 79
Setting, best hens for, 19
   Eggs, 19
Shape of permanent aviary, 4
Shells, supplying material to make, 20
Shelter for laying hens, 17
Shrubs, planting, in front of permanent aviaries, 7

Siamese Firebacks, 50
   Colours of cocks, 50
   Colours of hens, 50
   How to keep, 50
   Introduction of, 50
   Shyness and restlessness of, 50
Silvers, 37
   Colours of cocks, 37
   Colours of hens, 37
   Domesticity of, 38
   Introduction of, 37
   Longevity of, in confinement, 38
   Number of hens to cock, 38
   Points recommending, 37
   Pugnacity of cocks, 38
Sitting-box, 20
Sitting-boxes, ventilating, 23
"Sitting-hen Record," 22
Sitting-hens, tethering, 22
   Treatment of, 20
Sœmmerring cocks destroying their hens, how to prevent, 89
Sœmmerrings, 44
   Colours of cocks, 44
   Colours of hens, 45
   Domesticity of, 45
   Introduction of, 44
   Japanese name for, 44
   Number of hens to cock, 45
   Pugnacity of males, 44
Soft eggs, cause of, 81
Soiled boards in coops, how best to change, 15
Soil for permanent aviary, 4
Soiling from broken eggs, 23
Snow, birds able to withstand, 8
Space required to keep a pair of pheasants, small, 2
Span-roof aviary, permanent, 5
Stock, when to obtain, 16
Suburban houses, adaptability of pheasants for breeding and rearing in the grounds of, 1
Swinging birds by the legs, cruelty of, 82
Swinhoes, 42
   Beauty of, 42
   Colours of cocks, 42
   Colours of hens, 42
   Introduction of, 42

Swinhoes, number of eggs laid by hen, 43
    Number of hens to cock, 43
    Treatment required for, 42
    Unpopularity of, 43

T.

Testing eggs for fertility, 25
Thaumalea Amherstiæ, 39
    Picta, 34
Tonic for drinking-water, 17
Tyrannical nature of Lady Amherst cocks, 16

V.

Varied dispositions of my Versicolors, 86
Varieties, calls of the different, 84
    Desirable for the game-preserver, 89
    For town residents, two of the best, 1

Versicolors, 54
    Beauty of, 55
    Colours of cocks, 55
    Colours of hens, 55
    Harsh notes of, 84
    Introduction of, 54
    Large feeders, 55
    Number of hens to cock, 56
    Pride of, 86
    Pugnacity of males during breeding season, 55
    Result of crossing, for size, 54
    Varied dispositions of my, 86

W.

Water for aviaries, 11
When and how to feed chickens, 30

Y.

Young birds, cutting the wings of, 31
    Birds, portable aviaries for, 12

Catalogue of Practical Handbooks Published by L. Upcott Gill, 170, Strand, London, W.C.

American Dainties, and How to Prepare Them. By an AMERICAN LADY. *In paper, price* 1s., *by post* 1s. 2d.

Angler, Book of the All-Round. A Comprehensive Treatise on Angling in both Fresh and Salt Water. In Four Divisions as named below. By JOHN BICKERDYKE. With over 220 Engravings. *In cloth, price* 5s. 6d., *by post* 5s. 10d.

 Angling for Coarse Fish. Bottom Fishing, according to the Methods in use on the Thames, Trent, Norfolk Broads, and elsewhere. Illustrated. *In paper, price* 1s., *by post* 1s. 2d.

 Angling for Pike. The most approved Methods of Fishing for Pike or Jack. New Edition, revised and enlarged. Profusely Illustrated. *In paper, price* 1s., *by post* 1s. 2d.; *cloth,* 2s. (uncut), *by post* 2s. 3d.

 Angling for Game Fish. The Various Methods of Fishing for Salmon; Moorland, Chalk-stream, and Thames Trout; Grayling and Char. Well Illustrated. *In paper, price* 1s. 6d., *by post* 1s. 9d.

 Angling in Salt Water. Sea Fishing with Rod and Line, from the Shore, Piers, Jetties, Rocks, and from Boats; together with Some Account of Hand-Lining. Over 50 Engravings. *In paper, price* 1s., *by post,* 1s. 2d.; *cloth,* 2s. (uncut), *by post* 2s. 3d.

Angler, The Modern. A Practical Handbook on all Kinds of Angling. By "OTTER." Well illustrated. New Edition. *In cloth, price* 2s. 6d., *by post* 2s. 9d.

Aquaria, Book of. A Practical Guide to the Construction, Arrangement, and Management of Freshwater and Marine Aquaria; containing Full Information as to the Plants, Weeds, Fish, Molluscs, Insects, &c., How and Where to Obtain Them, and How to Keep Them in Health. Illustrated. By REV. GREGORY C. BATEMAN, A.K.C., and REGINALD A. R. BENNETT, B.A. *In cloth gilt, price* 5s. 6d., *by post* 5s. 10d.

Aquaria, Freshwater: Their Construction, Arrangement, Stocking, and Management. Fully Illustrated. By REV. G. C. BATEMAN, A.K.C. *In cloth gilt, price* 3s. 6d., *by post* 3s. 10d.

Aquaria, Marine: Their Construction, Arrangement, and Management. Fully Illustrated. By R. A. R. BENNETT, B.A. *In cloth gilt, price* 2s. 6d., *by post* 2s. 9d.

Australia, Shall I Try? A Guide to the Australian Colonies for the Emigrant Settler and Business Man. With two Illustrations. By GEORGE LACON JAMES. *In cloth gilt, price* 3s. 6d., *by post* 3s. 10d.

Autograph Collecting: A Practical Manual for Amateurs and Historical Students, containing ample information on the Selection and Arrangement of Autographs, the Detection of Forged Specimens, &c., &c., to which are added numerous Facsimiles for Study and Reference, and an extensive Valuation Table of Autographs worth Collecting. By HENRY T. SCOTT, M.D., L.R.C.P., &c. *In leatherette gilt, price* 7s. 6d. nett, *by post* 7s. 10d.

Bazaars and Fancy Fairs: Their Organization and Management. A Secretary's *Vade Mecum.* By JOHN MUIR. *In paper, price* 1s., *by post* 1s. 2d.

Bees and Bee-Keeping: Scientific and Practical. By F. R. CHESHIRE, F.L.S., F.R.M.S., Lecturer on Apiculture at South Kensington. *In two vols., cloth gilt, price* 16s., *by post* 16s. 6d.

 Vol. I., Scientific. A complete Treatise on the Anatomy and Physiology of the Hive Bee. *In cloth gilt, price* 7s. 6d., *by post* 7s. 10d.

 Vol. II., Practical Management of Bees. An Exhaustive Treatise on Advanced Bee Culture. *In cloth gilt, price* 8s. 6d., *by post* 8s. 11d.

Bee-Keeping, Book of. A very practical and Complete Manual on the Proper Management of Bees, especially written for Beginners and Amateurs who have but a few Hives. Fully Illustrated. By W. B. WEBSTER, First-class Expert, B.B.K.A. *In paper, price* 1s., *by post* 1 2d.; *cloth,* 1s. 6d., *by post* 1s. 8d.

Begonia Culture, for Amateurs and Professionals. Containing Full Directions for the Successful Cultivation of the Begonia, under Glass and in the Open Air. Illustrated. By B. C. RAVENSCROFT. *In paper, price 1s., by post 1s. 2d.*

Bent Iron Work: A Practical Manual of Instruction for Amateurs in the Art and Craft of Making and Ornamenting Light Articles in imitation of the beautiful Mediæval and Italian Wrought Iron Work. By F. J. ERSKINE. Illustrated. *In paper, price 1s., by post 1s. 2d.*

Birds, British, for the Cage and Aviary. Illustrated. By DR. W. T. GREENE. [*In the press.*

Boat Building and Sailing, Practical. Containing Full Instructions for Designing and Building Punts, Skiffs, Canoes, Sailing Boats, &c. Particulars of the most suitable Sailing Boats and Yachts for Amateurs, and Instructions for their Proper Handling. Fully Illustrated with Designs and Working Diagrams. By ADRIAN NEISON, C.E., DIXON KEMP, A.I.N.A., and G. CHRISTOPHER DAVIES. *In one vol., cloth gilt, price 7s. 6d., by post 7s. 10d.*

Boat Building for Amateurs, Practical. Containing Full Instructions for Designing and Building Punts, Skiffs, Canoes, Sailing Boats, &c. Fully Illustrated with Working Diagrams. By ADRIAN NEISON, C.E. Second Edition, Revised and Enlarged by DIXON KEMP, Author of "Yacht Designing," "A Manual of Yacht and Boat Sailing," &c. *In cloth gilt, price 2s. 6d. by post 2s. 9d.*

Boat Sailing for Amateurs, Practical. Containing Particulars of the most Suitable Sailing Boats and Yachts for Amateurs, and Instructions for their Proper Handling, &c. Illustrated with numerous Diagrams. By G. CHRISTOPHER DAVIES. Second Edition, Revised and Enlarged, and with several New Plans of Yachts. *In cloth gilt, price 5s., by post 5s. 4d.*

Bookbinding for Amateurs: Being Descriptions of the various Tools and Appliances Required, and Minute Instructions for their Effective Use. By W. J. E. CRANE. Illustrated with 156 Engravings. *In cloth gilt, price 2s. 6d., by post 2s. 9d.*

Bulb Culture, Popular. A Practical and Handy Guide to the Successful Cultivation of Bulbous Plants, both in the Open and under Glass. By W. D. DRURY. Fully Illustrated. *In paper, price 1s., by post 1s. 2d.*

Bunkum Entertainments: A Collection of Original Laughable Skits on Conjuring, Physiognomy, Juggling, Performing Fleas, Waxworks, Panorama, Phrenology, Phonograph, Second Sight, Lightning Calculators, Ventriloquism, Spiritualism, &c., to which are added Humorous Sketches, Whimsical Recitals, and Drawing-room Comedies. *In cloth, price 2s. 6d., by post 2s. 9d.*

Butterflies, The Book of British: A Practical Manual for Collectors and Naturalists. Splendidly Illustrated throughout with very accurate Engravings of the Caterpillars, Chrysalids, and Butterflies, both upper and under sides, from drawings by the Author or direct from Nature. By W. J. LUCAS, B.A. *Price 3s. 6d., by post 3s. 9d.*

Butterfly and Moth Collecting: Where to Search, and What to Do. By G. E. SIMMS. Illustrated. *In paper, price 1s., by post 1s. 2d.*

Cabinet Making for Amateurs. Being clear Directions How to Construct many Useful Articles, such as Brackets, Sideboard, Tables, Cupboards, and other Furniture. Illustrated. *In cloth gilt, price 2s. 6d., by post 2s. 9d.*

Cactus Culture for Amateurs: Being Descriptions of the various Cactuses grown in this country; with Full and Practical Instructions for their Successful Cultivation. By W. WATSON, Assistant Curator of the Royal Botanic Gardens, Kew. Profusely Illustrated. *In cloth, gilt, price 5s. nett, by post 5s. 4d.*

Cage Birds, Diseases of: Their Causes, Symptoms, and Treatment. A Handbook for everyone who keeps a Bird. By DR. W. T. GREENE, F.Z.S. *In paper, price 1s., by post 1s. 2d.*

Canary Book. The Breeding, Rearing, and Management of all Varieties of Canaries and Canary Mules, and all other matters connected with this Fancy. By ROBERT L. WALLACE. Third Edition. *In cloth gilt, price 5s., by post 5s. 4d.; with COLOURED PLATES, 6s. 6d., by post 6s. 10d.*

General Management of Canaries. Cages and Cage-making, Breeding, Managing, Mule Breeding, Diseases and their Treatment, Moulting, Pests, &c. Illustrated. *In cloth, price 2s. 6d., by post 2s. 9d.*

Exhibition Canaries. Full Particulars of all the different Varieties, their Points of Excellence, Preparing Birds for Exhibition, Format on and Management of Canary Societies and Exhibitions. Illustrated. *In cloth, price 2s. 6d., by post 2s. 9d.*

Cane Basket Work: A Practical Manual on Weaving Useful and Fancy Baskets By ANNIE FIRTH. Illustrated. *In cloth gilt, price* 1s. 6d., *by post* 1s. 8d.

Card Conjuring: Being Tricks with Cards, and How to Perform Them By PROF. ELLIS STANYON. Illustrated, and in Coloured Wrapper. *Price* 1s. *by post* 1s. 2d.

Card Tricks, Book of, for Drawing-room and Stage Entertainments by Amateurs; with an exposure of Tricks as practised by Card Sharpers and Swindlers. Numerous Illustrations. By PROF. R. KUNARD. *In illustrated wrapper, price* 2s. 6d., *by post* 2s. 9d.

Carnation Culture, for Amateurs. The Culture of Carnations and Picotees of all Classes in the Open Ground and in Pots. Illustrated. By B. C. RAVENSCROFT. *In paper, price* 1s., *by post* 1s. 2d.

Cats, Domestic or Fancy: A Practical Treatise on their Antiquity, Domestication, Varieties, Breeding, Management, Diseases and Remedies, Exhibition and Judging. By JOHN JENNINGS. Illustrated. *In cloth, price* 2s. 6d., *by post* 2s. 9d.

Chrysanthemum Culture, for Amateurs and Professionals. Containing Full Directions for the Successful Cultivation of the Chrysanthemum for Exhibition and the Market. By B. C. RAVENSCROFT. New Edition. Illustrated. *In paper, price* 1s., *by post* 1s. 2d.

Chrysanthemum, The Show, and Its Cultivation. By C. SCOTT, of the Sheffield Chrysanthemum Society. *In paper, price* 6d., *by post* 7d.

Coins, a Guide to English Pattern, in Gold, Silver, Copper, and Pewter, from Edward I. to Victoria, with their Value. By the REV. G. F. CROWTHER, M.A. Illustrated. *In silver cloth, with gilt facsimiles of Coins, price* 5s., *by post* 5s. 3d.

Coins of Great Britain and Ireland, a Guide to the, in Gold, Silver, and Copper, from the Earliest Period to the Present Time, with their Value. By the late COLONEL W. STEWART THORBURN. Third Edition. Revised and Enlarged, by H. A. GRUEBER, F.S.A. Illustrated. *In cloth gilt, price* 10s. 6d *net, by post* 10s. 10d.

Cold Meat Cookery. A Handy Guide to making really tasty and much appreciated Dishes from Cold Meat. By MRS. J. E. DAVIDSON. *In paper, price* 1s., *by post* 1s. 2d.

Collie, The. Its History, Points, and Breeding. By HUGH DALZIEL, Illustrated with Coloured Frontispiece and Plates. *In paper, price* 1s., *by post* 1s. 2d.; *cloth*, 2s., *by post* 2s. 3d.

Collie Stud Book. Edited by HUGH DALZIEL. *Price* 3s. 6d. *each, by post* 3s. 9d. *each.*

   Vol. I., containing Pedigrees of 1308 of the best-known Dogs, traced to their most remote known ancestors; Show Record to Feb., 1890, &c.
   Vol. II. Pedigrees of 795 Dogs, Show Record, &c.
   Vol. III. Pedigrees of 786 Dogs, Show Record, &c.

Columbarium, Moore's. Reprinted Verbatim from the originial Edition of 1735, with a Brief Notice of the Author. By W. B. TEGETMEIER, F.Z.S., Member of the British Ornithologists' Union. *Price* 1s., *by post* 1s. 2d.

Conjuring, Book of Modern. A Practical Guide to Drawing-room and Stage Magic for Amateurs. By PROFESSOR R. KUNARD. Illustrated. *In illustrated wrapper, price* 2s. 6d., *by post* 2s. 9d.

Conjuring for Amateurs. A Practical Handbook on How to Perform a Number of Amusing Tricks. By PROF. ELLIS STANYON. *In paper, price* 1s., *by post* 1s. 2d.

Cookery, The Encyclopædia of Practical. A complete Dictionary of all pertaining to the Art of Cookery and Table Service. Edited by THEO. FRANCIS GARRETT, assisted by eminent Chefs de Cuisine and Confectioners. Profusely Illustrated with Coloured Plates and Engravings by HAROLD FURNESS, GEO. CRUIKSHANK, W. MUNN ANDREW, and others. *In* 2 *vols., demy* 4to., *half bound, cushion edges,* £3 3s.; *carriage free,* £3 5s.

Cookery for Amateurs; or, French Dishes for English Homes of all Classes. Includes Simple Cookery, Middle-class Cookery, Superior Cookery, Cookery for Invalids, and Breakfast and Luncheon Cookery. By MADAME VALÉRIE. Second Edition. *In paper, price* 1s., *by post* 1s. 2d.

Cucumber Culture for Amateurs. Including also Melons, Vegetable Marrows, and Gourds. Illustrated. By W. J. MAY. *In paper, price* 1s. *by post* 1s. 2d.

Cyclist's Route Map of England and Wales. Shows clearly all the Main, and most of the Cross, Roads, Railroads, and the Distances between the Chief Towns, as well as the Mileage from London. In addition to this, Routes of *Thirty of the Most Interesting Tours* are printed in red. Fourth Edition, thoroughly revised. The map is printed on specially prepared vellum paper, and is the fullest, handiest, and best up-to-date tourist's map in the market. *In cloth, price 1s., by post 1s. 2d.*

Designing, Harmonic and Keyboard. Explaining a System whereby an endless Variety of Most Beautiful Designs suited to numberless Manufactures may be obtained by Unskilled Persons from any Printed Music. Illustrated by Numerous Explanatory Diagrams and Illustrative Examples. By C. H. WILKINSON. *Demy 4to, price £2 2s. nett.*

Dogs, Breaking and Training: Being Concise Directions for the proper education of Dogs, both for the Field and for Companions. Second Edition. By "PATHFINDER." With Chapters by HUGH DALZIEL. Illustrated. *In cloth gilt, price 6s. 6d., by post 6s. 10d.*

Dogs, British, Ancient and Modern: Their Varieties, History, and Characteristics. By HUGH DALZIEL, assisted by Eminent Fanciers. Beautifully Illustrated with COLOURED PLATES and full-page Engravings of Dogs of the Day, with numerous smaller illustrations in the text. This is the fullest work on the various breeds of dogs kept in England. In three volumes, *demy 8vo, cloth gilt, price 10s. 6d. each, by post 11s. each.*
   Vol. I. Dogs Used in Field Sports.
   Vol. II. Dogs Useful to Man in other Work than Field Sports; House and Toy Dogs.
   Vol. III. Practical Kennel Management: A Complete Treatise on all Matters relating to the Proper Management of Dogs whether kept for the Show Bench, for the Field, or for Companions.

Dogs, Diseases of: Their Causes, Symptoms, and Treatment; Modes of Administering Medicines; Treatment in cases of Poisoning, &c. For the use of Amateurs. By HUGH DALZIEL. Fourth Edition. Entirely Re-written and brought up to Date. *In paper, price 1s., by post 1s. 2d.; in cloth gilt, 2s., by post 2s. 3d.*

Dog-Keeping, Popular: Being a Handy Guide to the General Managemen and Training of all Kinds of Dogs for Companions and Pets. By J. MAXTEE. Illustrated. *In paper, price 1s., by post 1s. 2d.*

Engravings and their Value. Containing a Dictionary of all the Greatest Engravers and their Works. By J. H. SLATER. New Edition, Revised and brought up to date, with latest Prices at Auction. *In cloth gilt, price 15s. nett, by post, 15s. 5d.*

Entertainments, Amateur, for Charitable and other Objects: How to Organise and Work them with Profit and Success. By ROBERT GANTHONY. *In coloured cover, price 1s., by post 1s. 2d.*

Fancy Work Series, Artistic. A Series of Illustrated Manuals on Artistic and Popular Fancy Work of various kinds. Each number is complete in itself, and issued at the uniform *price of 6d., by post 7d.* Now ready—(1) MACRAMÉ LACE (Second Edition); (2) PATCHWORK; (3) TATTING; (4) CREWEL WORK; (5) APPLIQUÉ; (6) FANCY NETTING.

Feathered Friends, Old and New. Being the Experience of many years' Observation of the Habits of British and Foreign Cage Birds. By DR. W. T. GREENE. Illustrated. *In cloth gilt, price 5s., by post 5s. 4d.*

Ferns, The Book of Choice: for the Garden, Conservatory, and Stove. Describing the best and most striking Ferns and Selaginellas, and giving explicit directions for their Cultivation, the formation of Rockeries, the arrangement of Ferneries, &c. By GEORGE SCHNEIDER. With numerous Coloured Plates and other Illustrations. *In 3 vols., large post 4to. Cloth gilt, price £3 3s. nett, by post £3 5s.*

Ferns, Choice British. Descriptive of the most beautiful Variations from the common forms, and their Culture. By C. T. DRUERY, F.L.S. Very accurate PLATES, and other Illustrations. *In cloth gilt, price 2s. 6d., by post 2s. 9d.*

Ferrets and Ferreting. Containing Instructions for the Breeding, Management, and Working of Ferrets. Second Edition, Re-written and greatly Enlarged. Illustrated. *In paper, price 6d., by post 7d.*

Fertility of Eggs Certificate. These are Forms of Guarantee given by the Sellers to the Buyers of Eggs for Hatching, undertaking to refund value of any unfertile eggs, or to replace them with good ones. Very valuable to sellers of eggs, as they induce purchases. *In books, with counterfoils, price 6d., by post 7d.*

Firework Making for Amateurs. A complete, accurate, and easily understood work on Making Simple and High-class Fireworks. By DR. W. H. BROWNE, M.A. *In coloured wrapper, price 2s. 6d., by post 2s. 9d.*

Fisherman, The Practical. Dealing with the Natural History, the Legendary Lore, the Capture of British Fresh-Water Fish, and Tackle and Tackle-making. By J. H. KEENE. *In cloth gilt, price 7s. 6d., by post 7s. 10d.*

Fish Flesh, and Fowl When in Season, How to Select, Cook, and Serve. By MARY BARRETT BROWN. *In coloured wrapper, price 1s., by post 1s. 3d.*

Foreign Birds, Favourite, for Cages and Aviaries. How to Keep them in Health. Fully Illustrated. By W. T. GREENE, M.A., M.D., F.Z.S., &c. *In cloth, price 2s. 6d., by post 2s. 9d.*

Fox Terrier, The. Its History, Points, Breeding, Rearing, Preparing for Exhibition, and Coursing. By HUGH DALZIEL. Illustrated with Coloured Frontispiece and Plates. *In paper, price 1s., by post 1s. 2d.; cloth, 2s., by post 2s. 3d.*

Fox Terrier Stud Book. Edited by HUGH DALZIEL. *Price 3s. 6d. each, by post 3s. 9d. each.*
 Vol. I., containing Pedigrees of over 1400 of the best-known Dogs, traced to their most remote known ancestors.
 Vol. II. Pedigrees of 1544 Dogs, Show Record, &c.
 Vol. III. Pedigrees of 1214 Dogs, Show Record, &c.
 Vol. IV. Pedigrees of 1168 Dogs, Show Record, &c.
 Vol. V.   Pedigrees of 1662 Dogs, Show Record, &c.

Fretwork and Marquetry. A Practical Manual of Instructions in the Art of Fret-cutting and Marquetry Work. Profusely Illustrated. By D. DENNING. *In cloth, price 2s. 6d., by post 2s. 9d.*

Friesland Meres, A Cruise on the. By ERNEST R. SUFFLING. Illustrated. *In paper, price 1s., by post 1s. 2d.*

Fruit Culture for Amateurs. By S. T. WRIGHT. With Chapters on Insect and other Fruit Pests by W. D. DRURY. Illustrated. *In cloth gilt, price 3s. 6d., by post 3s. 9d.*

Game Preserving, Practical. Containing the fullest Directions for Rearing and Preserving both Winged and Ground Game, and Destroying Vermin; with other Information of Value to the Game Preserver. By W. CARNEGIE. Illustrated. *In cloth gilt, demy 8vo, price 21s., by post 21s. 5d.*

Games, the Book of a Hundred. By MARY WHITE. These Games are for Adults, and will be found extremely serviceable for Parlour Entertainment. They are Clearly Explained, are Ingenious, Clever, Amusing, and exceedingly Novel. *In stiff boards, price 2s. 6d. by post 2s. 9d.*

Gardening, Dictionary of. A Practical Encyclopædia of Horticulture, for Amateurs and Professionals. Illustrated with 2440 Engravings. Edited by G. NICHOLSON, Curator of the Royal Botanic Gardens, Kew; assisted by Prof. Trail, M.D., Rev. P. W. Myles, B.A., F.L.S., W. Watson, J. Garrett, and other Specialists. *In 4 vols., large post 4to. In cloth gilt, price £3, by post £3 2s.*

Gardening in Egypt. A Handbook of Gardening for Lower Egypt. With a Calendar of Work for the different Months of the Year. By WALTER DRAPER. *In cloth, price 3s. 6d., by post 3s. 9d.*

Gardening, Home. A Manual for the Amateur, Containing Instructions for the Laying Out, Stocking, Cultivation, and Management of Small Gardens—Flower, Fruit, and Vegetable. By W. D. DRURY, F.R.H.S. Illustrated. *In coloured wrapper, price 1s., by post 1s. 2d.*

Goat, Book of the. Containing Full Particulars of the Various Breeds of Goats, and their Profitable Management. With many Plates. By H. STEPHEN HOLMES PEGLER. Third Edition, with Engravings and Coloured Frontispiece. *In cloth gilt, price 4s. 6d., by post 4s. 10d.*

Goat-Keeping for Amateurs: Being the Practical Management of Goats for Milking Purposes. Abridged from "The Book of the Goat." Illustrated. *In paper, price 1s., by post 1s. 2d.*

Grape Growing for Amateurs. A Thoroughly Practical Book on Successful Vine Culture. By E. MOLYNEUX. Illustrated. *In paper, price 1s., by post 1s. 2d.*

Greenhouse Management for Amateurs. The Best Greenhouses and Frames, and How to Build and Heat them, Illustrated Descriptions of the most suitable Plants, with general and Special Cultural Directions, and all necessary information for the Guidance of the Amateur. Second Edition, Revised and Enlarged. Magnificently Illustrated. By W. J. MAY. *In cloth gilt, price 5s., by post 5s. 4d.*

Greyhound, The: Its History, Points, Breeding, Rearing, Training, and Running. By HUGH DALZIEL. With Coloured Frontispiece. *In cloth gilt, demy 8vo., price 2s. 6d., by post 2s. 9d.*

Guinea Pig, The, for Food, Fur, and Fancy. Its Varieties and its Management. By C. CUMBERLAND, F.Z.S. Illustrated. *In coloured wrapper, price 1s., by post 1s. 2d. In cloth gilt, with coloured frontispiece, price 2s. 6d., by post 2s. 9d.*

Handwriting, Character Indicated by. With Illustrations in Support of the Theories advanced, taken from Autograph Letters, of Statesmen, Lawyers, Soldiers, Ecclesiastics, Authors, Poets, Musicians, Actors, and the persons. Second Edition. By R. BAUGHAN. *In cloth gilt, price 2s 6d., by post 2s. 9d.*

Hardy Perennials and Old-fashioned Garden Flowers. Descriptions, alphabetically arranged, of the most desirable Plants for Borders, Rockeries, and Shrubberies, including Foliage as well as Flowering Plants. By J. WOOD. Profusely Illustrated. *In cloth, price 3s. 6d., by post 3s. 9d.*

Hawk Moths, Book of British. A Popular and Practical Manual for all Lepidopterists. Copiously illustrated in black and white from the Author's own exquisite Drawings from Nature. By W. J. LUCAS, B.A. *In cloth, price 3s. 6d., by post 3s. 9d.*

Home Medicine and Surgery: A Dictionary of Diseases and Accidents, and their proper Home Treatment. For Family Use. By W. J. MACKENZIE, M.D. Illustrated. *In cloth, price 2s. 6d., by post 2s, 9d.*

Horse-Keeper, The Practical. By GEORGE FLEMING, C.B., LL.D., F.R.C.V.S., late Principal Veterinary Surgeon to the British Army, and Ex-President of the Royal College of Veterinary Surgeons. *In cloth, price 3s. 6d., by post 3s. 10d.*

Horse-Keeping for Amateurs. A Practical Manual on the Management of Horses, for the guidance of those who keep one or two for their personal use. By FOX RUSSELL. *In paper, price 1s., by post 1s. 2d.; cloth 2s., by post 2s. 3d.*

Horses, Diseases of: Their Causes, Symptoms, and Treatment. For the use of Amateurs. By HUGH DALZIEL. *In paper, price 1s., by post 1s. 2d.; cloth 2s., by post 2s. 3d.*

Incubators and their Management. By J. H. SUTCLIFFE. New Edition, Revised and Enlarged. Illustrated. *In paper, price 1s., by post 1s. 2d.*

Inland Watering Places. A Description of the Spas of Great Britain and Ireland, their Mineral Waters, and their Medicinal Value, and the attractions which they offer to Invalids and other Visitors. Profusely illustrated. A Companion Volume to "Seaside Watering Places." *In cloth, price 2s. 6d., by post 2s. 10d*

Jack All Alone. Being a Collection of Descriptive Yachting Reminiscences. By FRANK COWPER, B.A., Author of "Sailing Tours." Illustrated. *In cloth gilt, price 3s. 6d., by post 3s. 10d.*

Journalism, Practical: How to Enter Thereon and Succeed. A book for all who think of "writing for the Press." By JOHN DAWSON. *In cloth gilt, price 2s. 6d., by post 2s. 9d.*

Laying Hens, How to Keep and to Rear Chickens in Large or Small Numbers, in Absolute Confinement, with Perfect Success. By MAJOR G. F. MORANT. *In paper, price 6d., by post 7d.*

Library Manual, The. A Guide to the Formation of a Library, and the Values of Rare and Standard Books. By J. H. SLATER, Barrister-at-Law. Third Edition. Revised and Greatly Enlarged. *In cloth gilt, price 7s. 6d. nett, by post 7s. 10d.*

Magic Lanterns, Modern. A Guide to the Management of the Optical Lantern, for the Use of Entertainers, Lecturers, Photograpers, Teachers, and others. By R. CHILD BAYLEY. *In paper, price 1s., by post 1s. 2d.*

Mice, Fancy: Their Varieties, Management, and Breeding. Third Edition, with additional matter and Illustrations. *In coloured wrapper representing different varieties, price 1s., by post 1s. 2d.*

Millinery, Handbook of. A Practical Manual of Instruction for Ladies. Illustrated. By MME. ROSÉE, Court Milliner, Principal of the School of Millinery. *In paper, price 1s., by post 1s. 2d.*

Model Yachts and Boats: Their Designing, Making, and Sailing. Illustrated with 118 Designs and Working Diagrams. By J. DU V. GROSVENOR. *In leatherette, price 5s., by post 5s. 3d.*

Monkeys, Pet, and How to Manage Them. Illustrated. By ARTHUR PATTERSON. *In cloth gilt, price 2s. 6d., by post 2s. 9d.*

Mountaineering, Welsh. A Complete and Handy Guide to all the Best Roads and Bye-Paths by which the Tourist should Ascend the Welsh Mountains. By A. W. PERRY. With numerous Maps. *In cloth gilt, price 2s. 6d., by post 2s. 9d.*

Mushroom Culture for Amateurs. With Full Directions for Successful Growth in Houses, Sheds, Cellars, and Pots, on Shelves, and Out of Doors. Illustrated. By W. J. MAY. *In paper, price 1s., by post 1s. 2d.*

Natural History Sketches among the Carnivora—Wild and Domesticated; with Observations on their Habits and Mental Faculties. By ARTHUR NICOLS, F.G.S., F.R.G.S. Illustrated. *In cloth gilt, price 2s. 6d., by post 2s. 9d.*

Naturalist's Directory, The, for 1898 (fourth year of issue). Invaluable to all Students and Collectors. *In paper, price 1s., by post 1s. 1d.*

Needlework, Dictionary of. An Encyclopædia of Artistic, Plain, and Fancy Needlework; Plain, practical, complete, and magnificently Illustrated. By S. F. A. CAULFEILD and B. C. SAWARD. *In demy 4to, 528pp, 829 Illustrations, extra cloth gilt, plain edges, cushioned bevelled boards, price 21s. nett, by post 21s. 9d.; with COLOURED PLATES, elegant satin brocade cloth binding, and coloured edges, 31s. 6d. nett, by post 32s.*

Orchids: Their Culture and Management, with Descriptions of all the Kinds in General Cultivation. Illustrated by Coloured Plates and Engravings. By W. WATSON, Assistant-Curator, Royal Botanic Gardens, Kew; Assisted by W. BEAN, Foreman, Royal Gardens, Kew. Second Edition, Revised and with Extra Plates. *In cloth gilt and gilt edges, price £1 1s. nett, by post £1 1s. 6d.*

Painters and Their Works. A Work of the Greatest Value to Collectors and such as are interested in the Art, as it gives, besides Biographical Sketches of all the Artists of Repute (not now living) from the 13th Century to the present date, the Market Value of the Principal Works Painted by Them, with Full Descriptions of Same. *In 3 vols., cloth, price 15s. nett per vol., by post 15s. 5d., or 37s. 6d. nett the set of 3, by post 38s. 3d.*

Painting, Decorative. A practical Handbook on Painting and Etching upon Textiles, Pottery, Porcelain, Paper, Vellum, Leather, Glass, Wood, Stone, Metals, and Plaster, for the Decoration of our Homes. By B. C. SAWARD. *In cloth gilt, price 3s. 6d., by post 3s. 9d.*

Parcel Post Dispatch Book (registered). An invaluable book for all who send parcels by post. Provides Address Labels, Certificate of Posting, and Record of Parcels Dispatched. By the use of this book parcels are insured against loss or damage to the extent of £2. Authorised by the Post Office. *Price 1s., by post 1s. 2d., for 100 parcels; larger sizes if required.*

Parrakeets, Popular. How to Keep and Breed Them. By DR. W. T. GREENE, M.D., M.A., F.Z.S., &c. *In coloured wrapper, price 1s., by post, 1s. 2d.*

Parrot, The Grey, and How to Treat it. By W. T. GREENE, M.D., M.A., F.Z.S., &c. *In coloured wrapper, price 1s., by post 1s. 2d.*

Parrots, the Speaking. The Art of Keeping and Breeding the principal Talking Parrots in Confinement. By DR. KARL RUSS. Illustrated with COLOURED PLATES and Engravings. *In cloth gilt, price 5s., by post 5s. 4d.*

Patience, Games of, for one or more Players. How to Play 142 different Games of Patience. By M. WHITMORE JONES. Illustrated. Series I., 39 games; Series II., 34 games; Series III., 35 games; Series IV., 37 games. Each 1s., by post 1s. 2d. *The four bound together in cloth gilt, price 5s., by post 5s. 4d.*

Perspective, The Essentials of. With numerous Illustrations drawn by the Author. By L. W. MILLER, Principal of the School of Industrial Art of the Pennsylvania Museum, Philadelphia. *Price 6s. 6d., by post 6s. 10d.*

Pheasant-Keeping for Amateurs. A Practical Handbook on the Breeding, Rearing, and General Management of Fancy Pheasants in Confinement. By GEO. HORNE. Fully Illustrated. *In cloth gilt, price 3s. 6d., by post 3s. 9d.*

Photographic Printing Processes, Popular. A Practical Guide to Printing with Gelatino-Chloride, Artigue, Platinotype, Carbon, Bromide, Collodio-Chloride, Bichromated Gum, and other Sensitised Papers. Illustrated. By H. MACLEAN, F.R.P.S. *Price 2s. 6d., by post 2s. 10d.*

Photography (Modern) for Amateurs. New and Revised Edition. By J. EATON FEARN. *In paper, price 1s., by post 1s. 2d.*

Pianofortes, Tuning and Repairing. The Amateur's Guide to the Practical Management of a Piano without the intervention of a Professional. By CHARLES BABBINGTON. *In paper, price 6d., by post 6½d.*

Picture-Frame Making for Amateurs. Being Practical Instructions in the Making of various kinds of Frames for Paintings, Drawings, Photographs, and Engravings. Illustrated. By the REV. J. LUKIN. *In paper, price 1s., by post 1s 2d.*

Pig, Book of the. The Selection, Breeding, Feeding, and Management of the Pig; the Treatment of its Diseases; the Curing and Preserving of Hams, Bacon, and other Pork Foods; and other information appertaining to Pork Farming. By PROFESSOR JAMES LONG. Fully Illustrated with Portraits of Prize Pigs, Plans of Model Piggeries, &c. *In cloth gilt, price 10s. 6d., by post 10s. 11d.*

Pig-Keeping, Practical: A Manual for Amateurs, based on personal Experience in Breeding, Feeding, and Fattening; also in Buying and Selling Pigs at Market Prices. By R. D. GARRATT. *In paper, price 1s., by post 1s. 2d.*

Pigeons, Fancy. Containing full Directions for the Breeding and Management of Fancy Pigeons, and Descriptions of every known Variety, together with all other information of interest or use to Pigeon Fanciers. Third Edition. 18 COLOURED PLATES, and 22 other full-page Illustrations. By J. C. LYELL. *In cloth gilt, price 10s. 6d., by post 10s. 10d.*

Pigeon-Keeping for Amateurs. A Complete Guide to the Amateur Breeder of Domestic and Fancy Pigeons. By J. C. LYELL. Illustrated. *In cloth, price 2s. 6d., by post 2s. 9d.*

Polishes and Stains for Wood: A Complete Guide to Polishing Woodwork, with Directions for Staining, and Full Information for Making the Stains, Polishes, &c., in the simplest and most satisfactory manner. By DAVID DENNING. *In paper, 1s., by post 1s. 2d.*

Pool, Games of. Describing Various English and American Pool Games, and giving the Rules in full. Illustrated *In paper, price 1s., by post 1s. 2d.*

Postage Stamps, and their Collection. A Practical Handbook for Collectors of Postal Stamps, Envelopes, Wrappers, and Cards. By OLIVER FIRTH, Member of the Philatelic Societies of London, Leeds, and Bradford. Profusely Illustrated. *In cloth gilt, price 3s. 6d., by post 3s. 10d.*

Postage Stamps of Europe, The Adhesive: A Practical Guide to their Collection, Identification, and Classification. Especially designed for the use of those commencing the Study. By W. A. S. WESTOBY. Beautifully Illustrated. *In Parts, 1s. each, by post 1s. 2d.*

Postmarks, History of British. With 350 Illustrations and a List of Numbers used in Obliterations. By J. H. DANIELS. *In cloth, price 2s. 6d., by post 2s. 9d.*

Pottery and Porcelain, English. A Guide for Collectors. Handsomely Illustrated with Engravings of Specimen Pieces and the Marks used by the different Makers. New Edition, Revised and Enlarged. By the REV. E. A. DOWNMAN. *In cloth gilt, price 5s., by post 5s. 3d.*

Poultry-Farming, Profitable. Describing in Detail the Methods that Give the Best Results, and pointing out the Mistakes to be Avoided. Illustrated. By J. H. SUTCLIFFE. *Price 1s., by post 1s. 2d.*

Poultry-Keeping, Popular. A Practical and Complete Guide to Breeding and Keeping Poultry for Eggs or for the Table. By F. A. MACKENZIE. Illustrated. *In paper, price 1s., by post 1s. 2d.*

Poultry and Pigeon Diseases Their Causes, Symptoms, and Treatment. A Practical Manual for all Fanciers. By QUINTIN CRAIG and JAMES LYELL. *In paper, price 1s., by post 1s. 2d.*

Poultry for Prizes and Profit. Contains: Breeding Poultry for Prizes, Exhibition Poultry and Management of the Poultry Yard. Handsomely Illustrated. Second Edition. By PROF. JAMES LONG. *In cloth gilt, price 2s. 6d., by post 2s. 10d.*

Rabbit, Book of The. A Complete Work on Breeding and Rearing all Varieties of Fancy Rabbits, giving their History, Variations, Uses, Points, Selection, Mating, Management, &c., &c. SECOND EDITION. Edited by KEMPSTER W. KNIGHT. Illustrated with Coloured and other Plates. *In cloth gilt, price 10s. 6d., by post 10s. 11d.*

Rabbits, Diseases of: Their Causes, Symptoms, and Cure. With a Chapter on THE DISEASES OF CAVIES. Reprinted from "The Book of the Rabbit" and "The Guinea Pig for Food, Fur and Fancy." *In paper, price 1s., by post 1s. 2d.*

Rabbits for Prizes and Profit. The Proper Management of Fancy Rabbits in Health and Disease, for Pets or the Market, and Descriptions of every known Variety, with Instructions for Breeding Good Specimens. Illustrated. By CHARLES RAYSON. *In cloth gilt, price 2s. 6d., by post 2s. 9d.* Also in Sections, as follows:

> *General Management of Rabbits.* Including Hutches, Breeding, Feeding, Diseases and their Treatment, Rabbit Courts, &c. Fully Illustrated. *In paper, price 1s., by post 1s. 2d.*

> *Exhibition Rabbits.* Being descriptions of all Varieties of Fancy Rabbits, their Points of Excellence, and how to obtain them. Illustrated. *In paper, price 1s., by post 1s. 2d*

Road Charts (Registered). For Army Men, Volunteers, Cyclists, and other Road Users. By S. W. H. DIXON and A. B. H. CLERKE. No. 1.—London to Brighton. *Price 2d., by post 2½d.*

Roses for Amateurs. A Practical Guide to the Selection and Cultivation of the best Roses. Illustrated. By the REV. J. HONYWOOD D'OMBRAIN, Hon. Sec. Nat. Rose Soc. *In paper, price 1s., by post 1s. 2d.*

Sailing Guide to the Solent and Poole Harbour, with Practical Hints as to Living and Cooking on, and Working a Small Yacht. By LIEUT.-COL. T. G. CUTHELL. Illustrated with Coloured Charts. *In cloth gilt, price 2s. 6d., by post 2s. 9d.*

Sailing Tours. The Yachtman's Guide to the Cruising Waters of the English and Adjacent Coasts. With Descriptions of every Creek, Harbour, and Roadstead on the Course. With numerous Charts printed in Colours, showing Deep water, Shoals, and Sands exposed at low water, with sounding. *In Crown 8vo., cloth gilt.* By FRANK COWPER, B.A.

> *Vol. I.*, the Coasts of Essex and Suffolk, from the Thames to Aldborough. Six Charts. *Price 5s., by post 5s. 3d.*

> *Vol. II.* The South Coast, from the Thames to the Scilly Islands, twenty-five Charts. *Price 7s. 6d., by post 7s. 10d.*

> *Vol. III.* The Coast of Brittany, from L'Abervrach to St. Nazaire, and an Account of the Loire. Twelve Charts. *Price 7s. 6d., by post 7s. 10d.*

> *Vol. IV.* The West Coast, from Land's End to Mull of Galloway, including the East Coast of Ireland. Thirty Charts. *Price 10s. 6d., by post 10s. 10d.*

> *Vol. V.* The Coasts of Scotland and the N.E. of England down to Aldborough. Forty Charts. *Price 10s. 6d., by post 10s. 10d.*

St. Bernard, The. Its History, Points, Breeding, and Rearing. By HUGH DALZIEL. Illustrated with Coloured Frontispiece and Plates. *In cloth, price 2s 6d., by post 2s. 9d.*

St. Bernard Stud Book. Edited by HUGH DALZIEL. *Price 3s. 6d. each, by post 3s. 9d. each.*

> *Vol. I.* Pedigrees of 1278 of the best known Dogs traced to their most remote known ancestors, Show Record, &c.

> *Vol. II.* Pedigrees of 564 Dogs, Show Record, &c.

Sea-Fishing for Amateurs. Practical Instructions to Visitors at Seaside Places for Catching Sea-Fish from Pier-heads, Shore, or Boats, principally by means of Hand Lines, with a very useful List of Fishing Stations, the Fish to be caught there, and the Best Seasons. By FRANK HUDSON. Illustrated. *In paper, price 1s., by post 1s. 2d.*

Sea-Fishing on the English Coast. The Art of Making and Using Sea-Tackle, with a full account of the methods in vogue during each month of the year, and a Detailed Guide for Sea-Fishermen to all the most Popular Watering Places on the English Coast. By F. G. AFLALO. Illustrated. *In cloth gilt, price 2s. 6d., by post 2s. 9d.*

Sea-Life, Realities of. Describing the Duties, Prospects, and Pleasures of a Young Sailor in the Mercantile Marine. By H. E. ACRAMAN COATE. With a Preface by J. R. DIGGLE, M.A., M.L.S.B. *In cloth, price 3s. 6d., by post 3s. 10d.*

Seaside Watering Places. A Description of the Holiday Resorts on the Coasts of England and Wales, the Channel Islands, and the Isle of Man, giving full particulars of them and their attractions, and all information likely to assist persons in selecting places in which to spend their Holidays according to their individual tastes. Illustrated. Twenty-second Year of Issue. Ready in May. *In cloth, price 2s. 6d., by post 2s. 10d.*

Sea Terms, a Dictionary of. For the use of Yachtsmen, Amateur Boatmen, and Beginners. By A. ANSTED. Fully Illustrated. *Cloth gilt, price 7s. 6d. net, by post 7s. 11d.*

Shadow Entertainments, and How to Work them: being Something about Shadows, and the way to make them Profitable and Funny. By A. PATTERSON. *In paper, price 1s., by post 1s. 2d.*

Shave, An Easy: The Mysteries, Secrets, and Whole Art of, laid bare for 1s., by post 1s. 2d. Edited by JOSEPH MORTON.

Sheet Metal, Working in: Being Practical Instructions for Making and Mending Small Articles in Tin, Copper, Iron, Zinc, and Brass. Illustrated. Third Edition. By the Rev. J. LUKIN, B.A. *In paper, price 1s., by post 1s. 1d.*

Shorthand, on Gurney's System (Improved), LESSONS IN: Being Instructions in the Art of Shorthand Writing as used in the Service of the two Houses of Parliament. By R. E. MILLER. *In paper, price 1s., by post 1s. 2d.*

Shorthand, Exercises in, for Daily Half Hours, on a Newly-devised and Simple Method, free from the Labour of Learning. Illustrated. Being Part II. of "Lessons in Shorthand on Gurney's System (Improved)." By R. E. MILLER. *In paper, price 9d., by post 10d.*

Skating Cards: An Easy Method of Learning Figure Skating, as the Cards can be used on the Ice. *In cloth case, 2s. 6d., by post 2s. 9d.; leather, 3s. 6d., by post 3s. 9d.* A cheap form is issued printed on paper and made up as a small book, 1s., by post 1s. 1d.

Sleight of Hand. A Practical Manual of Legerdemain for Amateurs and Others. New Edition, Revised and Enlarged. Profusely Illustrated. By E. SACHS. *In cloth gilt, price 6s. 6d., by post 6s. 10d.*

Snakes, Marsupials, and Birds. A Charming Book of Anecdotes, Adventures, and Zoological Notes. A capital book for Boys. By ARTHUR NICOLS, F.G.S., F.R.G.S., &c. Illustrated. *In cloth gilt, price 3s. 6d., by post 3s. 10d.*

Taxidermy, Practical. A Manual of Instruction to the Amateur in Collecting, Preserving, and Setting-up Natural History Specimens of all kinds. With Examples and Working Diagrams. By MONTAGU BROWNE, F.Z.S., Curator of Leicester Museum. Second Edition. *In cloth gilt, price 7s. 6d., by post 7s. 10d.*

Thames Guide Book. From Lechlade to Richmond. For Boating Men, Anglers, Picnic Parties, and all Pleasure-seekers on the River. Arranged on an entirely new plan. Second Edition, profusely Illustrated. *In cloth, price 1s. 6d., by post 1s. 9d.*

Tomato and Fruit Growing as an Industry for Women. Lectures given at the Forestry Exhibition, Earl's Court, during July and August, 1893. By GRACE HARRIMAN, Practical Fruit Grower and County Council Lecturer. *In paper, price 1s., by post 1s. 1d.*

Tomato Culture for Amateurs. A Practical and very Complete Manual on the subject. By B. C. RAVENSCROFT. Illustrated. *In paper, price 1s., by post 1s. 1d.*

Trapping, Practical: Being some Papers on Traps and Trapping for Vermin, with a Chapter on General Bird Trapping and Snaring. By W. CARNEGIE. *In paper, price 1s., by post 1s. 2d.*

Turning for Amateurs: Being Descriptions of the Lathe and its Attachments and Tools, with minute Instructions for their Effective Use on Wood, Metal, Ivory, and other Materials. Second Edition, Revised and Enlarged. By JAMES LUKIN, B.A. Illustrated with 144 Engravings. *In cloth gilt, price 2s. 6d., by post 2s. 9d.*

Turning Lathes. A Manual for Technical Schools and Apprentices. A Guide to Turning, Screw-cutting, Metal-spinning, &c. Edited by JAMES LUKIN, B.A. Third Edition. With 194 Illustrations. *In cloth gilt, price 3s., by post 3s. 3d.*

Vamp, How to. A Practical Guide to the Accompaniment of Songs by the Unskilled Musician. With Examples. *In paper, price 9d., by post 10d.*

Vegetable Culture for Amateurs. Containing Concise Directions for the Cultivation of Vegetables in small Gardens so as to insure Good Crops. With Lists of the Best Varieties of each Sort. By W. J. MAY. Illustrated. *In paper, price 1s., by post 1s. 2d.*

Ventriloquism, Practical. A thoroughly reliable Guide to the Art of Voice Throwing and Vocal Mimicry, Vocal Instrumentation, Ventriloquial Figures, Entertaining, &c. By ROBERT GANTHONY. Numerous Illustrations. *In cloth gilt, price 2s. 6d., by post 2s. 9d.*

Violins (Old) and their Makers: Including some References to those of Modern Times. By JAMES M. FLEMING. Illustrated with Facsimiles of Tickets, Sound-Holes, &c. *In cloth gilt, price 6s. 6d. nett, by post 6s. 10d.*

Violin School, Practical, for Home Students. Instructions and Exercises in Violin Playing, for the use of Amateurs, Self-learners, Teachers, and others. With a Supplement on "Easy Legato Studies for the Violin." By J. M. FLEMING. *Demy 4to, cloth gilt, price 9s. 6d., by post 10s. 2d.* Without Supplement, *price 7s. 6d., by post 8s.*

Vivarium, The. Being a Full Description of the most Interesting Snakes, Lizards, and other Reptiles, and How to Keep Them Satisfactorily in Confinement. By REV. G. C. BATEMAN. Beautifully Illustrated. *In cloth gilt, price 7s. 6d. nett, by post 8s.*

War Medals and Decorations. A Manual for Collectors, with some account of Civil Rewards for Valour. Beautifully Illustrated. By D. HASTINGS IRWIN. *In cloth gilt, price 7s. 6d., by post 7s. 10d.*

Whippet and Race-Dog, The: How to Breed, Rear, Train, Race, and Exhibit the Whippet, the Management of Race Meetings, and Original Plans of Courses. By FREEMAN LLOYD. *In cloth gilt, price 3s. 6d., by post 3s. 10d.*

Whist, Modern Scientific. A Practical Manual on new Lines, and with Illustrative Hands, printed in Colour. By C. J. MELROSE. *In cloth gilt, price 6s., by post 6s. 5d.*

Wildfowling, Practical: A Book on Wildfowl in Wildfowl Shooting. By HY. SHARP. The result of 25 years' experience Wildfowl Shooting under all sorts of conditions of locality as well as circumstances. Profusely Illustrated. *Demy 8vo, cloth gilt, price 12s. 6d. nett, by post 12s. 10d.*

Wild Sports in Ireland. Being Picturesque and Entertaining Descriptions of several visits paid to Ireland, with Practical Hints likely to be of service to the Angler, Wildfowler, and Yachtsman. By JOHN BICKERDYKE, Author of "The Book of the All-Round Angler," &c. Beautifully Illustrated from Photographs taken by the Author. *In cloth gilt, price 6s., by post 6s. 4d.*

Window Ticket Writing. Containing full Instructions on the Method of Mixing and Using the Various Inks, &c., required, Hints on Stencilling as applied to Ticket Writing, together with Lessons on Glass Writing, Japanning on Tin, &c. Especially written for the use of Learners and Shop Assistants. By WM. C. SCOTT. *In paper, price 1s., by post 1s. 2d.*

Wire and Sheet Gauges of the World. Compared and Compiled by C. A. B. PFEILSCHMIDT, of Sheffield. *In paper, price 1s., by post 1s. 1d.*

Wood Carving for Amateurs. Full Instructions for producing all the different varieties of Carvings. SECOND EDITION. Edited by D. DENNING. *In paper, price 1s., by post 1s. 2d.*

Workshop Makeshifts. Being a Collection of Practical Hints and Suggestions for the use of Amateur Workers in Wood and Metal. Fully Illustrated. By H. J. S. CASSALL. *In cloth gilt, price 2s. 6d., by post 2s. 9d.*

FICTION LIBRARY.

Decameron of a Hypnotist. Tales of Dread. By E. SUFFLING, Author of "The Story Hunter," &c. With Illustrations. *Cloth gilt, 3s. 6d., by post 3s. 10d.*

CLASSIFICATION INDEX

ART.
	PAGE.
Designing	4
Old Violins	11
Painting	7
Perspective	7
Violin School	11

AMUSEMENTS.
Amateur Entertainments	4
Bunkum Entertainments	2
Card Conjuring	3
Card Tricks	3
Conjuring	3, 10
Games	5
Magic Lanterns	6
Patience	7
Pool	8
Shadow Entertainments	10
Sleight of Hand	10
Vamping	10
Ventriloquism	11
Whist	11

COLLECTORS.
Autograph	1
Books	6
Coins	3
Engravings	4
Handwriting	6
Library Manual	6
Painters	7
Postage Stamps	8
Postmarks	8
Pottery and Porcelain	8
Stamps of Europe	8
War Medals	11

DOGS & HORSES.
Breaking Dogs	4
British Dogs	4
Collie	3
Diseases of Dogs	4
Diseases of Horses	6
Dog-Keeping	4
Fox Terrier	5
Greyhound	5
Horse-Keeper	6
Horse-Keeping	6
St. Bernard	9
Whippet	11

FARM.
Goat-Keeping	5
Pig-Keeping	8
Poultry Farming	8

GARDENING.
	PAGE.
Begonia Culture	2
Bulb Culture	2
Cactus Culture	2
Carnation Culture	3
Chrysanthemum Culture	3
Cucumber Culture	3
Dictionary	5
Ferns	4
Fruit Culture	5
Gardening in Egypt	5
Grape Growing	5
Greenhouse Management	5
Hardy Perennials	6
Home	5
Mushroom Culture	7
Orchids	7
Roses	9
Tomato Culture	10
Tomato Growing	10
Vegetable Culture	10

HOME.
American Dainties	1
Cold Meat Cookery	3
Cookery	3
Fancy Work	4
Fish, Flesh, & Fowl	5
Home Medicine	6
Millinery	6
Needlework Dictionary	7
Shaving	10

MECHANICS.
Bent Ironwork	2
Boat Building	2
Bookbinding	2
Cabinet Making	2
Cane Basket Work	3
Firework Making	5
Fretwork	5
Marqueterie	5
Model Yachts	6
Piano Tuning	7
Picture-Frame Making	8
Sheet Metal Work	10
Ticket Writing	11
Turning	10
Turning Lathes	10
Wire Gauges	11
Wood Carving	11
Wood Polishes	8
Workshop Makeshifts	11

NATURAL HISTORY.
Aquaria	1

	PAGE.
Bees	1
Butterflies	2
Directory	7
Hawk Moths	6
Sketches	7
Snakes	10
Taxidermy	10
Vivarium	11

PETS.
British Birds	2
Cage Birds' Diseases	2
Canaries	2
Cats	3
Feathered Friends	4
Foreign Birds	5
Grey Parrots	7
Guinea Pig	6
Mice	6
Monkeys	6
Parrakeets	7
Pheasants	7
Rabbits	8
Speaking Parrots	7

POULTRY & PIGEONS.
Columbarium	3
Diseases	8
Fancy Pigeons	8
Incubators	6
Laying Hens	6
Pigeon-Keeping	8
Poultry-Farming	8
Poultry-Keeping	8

SPORT.
Angling	1, 5
Boat Building	2
Boat Sailing	2
Cycling Map	4, 9
Ferrets	4
Game Preserving	5
Sea-Fishing	1, 9
Skating	10
Trapping	10
Wildfowling	11
Wild Sports	11

TOURIST.
Friesland Meres	5
Inland Watering Places	6
Mountaineering	7
Road Chart	9
Sailing Tours	9
Seaside Watering Places	9
Solent Guide	9
Thames Guide	10

EXTRA SUPPLEMENTS *Well Illustrated.*
The Ladies', each Month, 1st Wed.; The Philatelists', 2nd Wed.; The Home, 3rd Wed.;

BARGAINS
in Everything and Anything are readily secured through *The Bazaar, Exchange and Mart* Newspaper, which is used by Private Persons for disposing of things they no longer require. **THE** paper for Buying, Selling, and Exchanging by Private Persons.

TELEGRAMS: "BAZAAR, LONDON."

2d. at Newsagents.

2d. at Bookstalls.

By post for 3 Stamps.

OFFICE: 170, STRAND, LONDON.

ADVICE
on every possible subject may be obtained on application to *The Bazaar, Exchange and Mart*, which has the largest staff of Eminent Experts of any paper in the Kingdom, and these Experts freely advise its readers. **THE** paper *par excellence* for Amateurs.

EXTRA SUPPLEMENTS—*continued.*
The Cyclists', each Month, 1st Mon.; The Sportsman's, 2nd Mon.; The Garden, 3rd Mon.; The Dog Owners', Last Mon.

PUBLISHED BY E. and F. N. SPON, Ltd.

Crown 4to, full gilt, fancy cloth, 478 pages Letterpress and 735 Engravings, price 7s. 6d.

POPULAR ENGINEERING:

BEING INTERESTING AND INSTRUCTIVE EXAMPLES IN

CIVIL, MECHANICAL, ELECTRICAL, CHEMICAL, MINING, MILITARY, and NAVAL ENGINEERING.

GRAPHICALLY AND PLAINLY DESCRIBED AND

Specially Written for those about to enter the Engineering Profession and the Scientific Amateur. With Chapters upon

PERPETUAL MOTION and ENGINEERING COLLEGES and SCHOOLS.

By F. DYE.

SPONS' MECHANICS' OWN BOOK:

A MANUAL FOR HANDICRAFTSMEN AND AMATEURS.

Complete in One large Vol., demy 8vo, cloth, containing 700 pp. and 1420 Illustrations. Fourth Edition, 6s.; or half-bound, French morocco, 7s. 6d.

Contents:

Mechanical Drawing; Casting and Founding in Iron, Brass, Bronze, and other Alloys; Forging and Finishing Iron; Sheet Metal Working; Soldering, Brazing, and Burning; Carpentry and Joinery, embracing descriptions of some 400 woods; over 200 Illustrations of Tools and their Uses; Explanations (with Diagrams) of 116 Joints and Hinges, and Details of Construction of Workshop Appliances; Rough Furniture, Garden and Yard Erections, and House-Building; Cabinet-making and Veneering; Carving and Fret-cutting; Upholstery; Painting, Graining, and Marbling; Staining Furniture, Woods, Floors, and Fittings; Gilding, Dead and Bright, on various Grounds; Polishing Marble, Metals and Wood; Varnishing; Mechanical Movements, illustrating contrivances for transmitting Motion; Turning in Wood and Metals; Masonry, embracing Stonework, Brickwork, Terra-cotta, and Concrete; Roofing with Thatch, Tiles, Slates, Felt, Zinc, &c.; Glazing with and without Putty, and Lead Glazing; Plastering and Whitewashing; Paperhanging; Gas-fitting; Bell-hanging, Ordinary and Electric Systems; Lighting; Warming; Ventilating; Roads, Pavements and Bridges; Hedges, Ditches and Drains; Water Supply and Sanitation; Hints on House Construction suited to New Countries.

SPONS' HOUSEHOLD MANUAL:

A TREASURY OF DOMESTIC RECEIPTS AND GUIDE FOR HOME MANAGEMENT.

Demy 8vo, cloth, containing 957 pp. and 250 Illustrations, price 7s. 6d.; or half-bound French morocco, 9s.

Principal Contents:

Hints for selecting a good House; Sanitation; Water Supply; Ventilation and Warming; Lighting; Furniture and Decoration; Thieves and Fire; The Larder; Curing Foods for lengthened Preservation; The Dairy; The Cellar; The Pantry; The Kitchen; Receipts for Dishes; The Housewife's Room; Housekeeping, Marketing; The Dining-room; The Drawing-room; The Bed-room; The Nursery; The Sick-room; The Bath-room; The Laundry; The School-room; The Playground; The Work-room; The Library; The Garden; The Farmyard; Small Motors; Household Law.

London: E. & F. N. SPON, Ltd., 125, Strand.

New York: SPON & CHAMBERLAIN, 12, Cortlandt Street.

Dean's Shilling Practical Guide Books.

POST FREE 1s. 1d. EACH.

Ailments of Poultry. By F. T. BARTON.

†Horses. The Gentleman's Guide. By JAMES MILLS, M.V.C.S. With suggestions relative to the treatment of Diseases of Horses, and the Art of Horsemanship, by RAREY. 21st Edition.

*Kennel Companion and Referee. By DR. GORDON STABLES. Illustrated.

*Pet Animals; or, the Amateur's Zoo. Their Habits, Characteristics, and How to Manage them in Captivity. By ARTHUR PATTERSON. With 40 Illustrations.

†The British Aviary; or, Song Birds. Containing Addenda on the various breeds of Canaries. By THOMAS ANDREWS. Coloured Frontispiece.

*Canaries. How to Breed, Rear, and Keep them in Health. With pictures of nineteen varieties, and chapter on Mules. By KARL RUSS.

†Parrots, Cockatoos, &c. By CAPTAIN BROWN. Forty Illustrations, by JOSEPH P. KIDD.

†Cage Birds. By BECHSTEIN (including Parrots). Fifty-six Illustrations. Edited by H. G. ADAMS.

‡Rabbit Keeper's Guide. How best to Rear, Feed, and Keep the several kinds of Rabbits.

*Pigeons. Their Varieties, Treatment, Breeding, and Diseases. By EDWARD BROWN, F.L.S. Illustrated by LUDLOW.

*Poultry. Their Varieties, Breeding, and Diseases. By EDWARD BROWN, F.L.S. Twenty-four Illustrations by LUDLOW.

Sheep. Their Varieties, Points, and Characteristics. By JOSEPH DARBY.

Cookery Made Easy. By a Lady. With Coloured Plates. 24th Edition.

Confectionery, Pastry, Preserving Sweets, &c. By GEORGE REID.

*Card Tricks and Conjuring Up-to-Date. By HERCAT.

Fireworks and Chemical Surprises. By CHARLES GILBERT.

*Crown 8vo. Illustrated. * Bound in Illustrated stiff varnished paper covers. † Bound in Illustrated stiff paper covers. ‡ Cloth bound, gilt lettering.*

LONDON: DEAN & SON, LIMITED, 160a, FLEET ST., E.C.

Entirely New Edition—Now Ready,
Showing the Very Latest Changes.

JOHNSTON'S
"MODERN" LIBRARY MAP of ENGLAND & WALES.

SIZE 68in. by 54½in.

On Cloth, Mahogany Rollers, bound with Silk up the sides, and Varnished, price £1 7s. 6d.; on Cloth, Stained Wood Rollers, and Varnished, price £1 1s.; also in 4 Sheets, size 35in. by 29½in., each price 2s. per sheet in Cloth Case; or 3s. 6d. per sheet on Cloth to fold, and in Cloth Case.

Also Third Edition,
W. & A. K. JOHNSTON'S
RAILWAY & CANAL MAP OF ENGLAND & WALES,

Showing each Railway System in a particular colour and marking. Size, 50in. by 42in. Price, in two sheets, 7s. 6d.; on Cloth, Rollers, and Varnished, 10s.; on Cloth to fold in Titled Cloth Case, 10s.

W. & A. K. JOHNSTON,
Edina Works, Easter Road, and 7, Hanover Street,
EDINBURGH;
5, White Hart Street, Warwick Lane, London, E.C.

DOG SOAP

MADE BY

SPRATT'S PATENT LIMITED.

A NON-POISONOUS PREPARATION.

Invaluable for Preparing the Coat for Exhibition

SOLD IN TABLETS.

DOG MEDICINES.

- Alterative Cooling Powders
- Aperient Tasteless Biscuits
- Chronic Skin Disease Cure
- Cough Pills
- Chemical Food
- Chorea Pills (St. Vitus' Dance)
- Diarrhœa Mixture
- Distemper Powders
- Distemper Pills
- Disinfectant for Kennels
- Ear Canker Lotion
- Eczema Lotion
- Eye Lotion
- Hair Stimulant
- Jaundice or "Yellows" Pills
- **Locurium Oil** (Patent) for Animal Use
- **Locurium Oil** (Patent) for Human Use (including Government Stamp)
- Mange Lotion
- Purging Pills
- Rheumatic and Sprain Liniment
- Rheumatic and Chest Founder Pills
- Tonic Condition Pills
- Vegetable Puppy Vermifuge
- Worm Powders
- Worm Pills

YOUR TRADESMAN OR STORES WILL SUPPLY YOU.

Spratt's Patent Limited, Bermondsey, London, S.E.

PAMPHLET ON CANINE DISEASES, POST FREE.

Printed in the United Kingdom
by Lightning Source UK Ltd.
135559UK00001B/77/P